The Distance from Slaughter County

The Distance from Slaughter County

Lessons from Flyover Country

STEVEN MOORE

THE UNIVERSITY OF NORTH CAROLINA PRESS

Chapel Hill

Designed by Jamison Cockerham
Set in Scala and Sentinel
by codeMantra

Manufactured in the United States of America

Cover art: Background wood paneling, © RyanJLane/istockphoto.com.
Cover design by Lindsay Starr.

LIBRARY OF CONGRESS CATALOGING-IN-PUBLICATION DATA
Names: Moore, Steven, 1987– author.
Title: The distance from Slaughter County : lessons
from flyover country / Steven Moore.
Description: Chapel Hill : The University of North Carolina
Press, [2023] | Includes bibliographical references.
Identifiers: LCCN 2022037860 | ISBN 9781469673950
(cloth ; alk. paper) | ISBN 9781469673967 (ebook)
Subjects: LCSH: National characteristics, American. |
United States—Rural conditions. | LCGFT: Essays.
Classification: LCC E169.1 .M7876 2023 | DDC 973—dc23/eng/20220822
LC record available at https://lccn.loc.gov/2022037860

CONTENTS

The Distance from Slaughter County

Where I Was From

I live in a college town in western Oregon and lately people here have been talking about their small-town midwestern upbringing like it was a war they barely survived. They feel the deep bruise when they move a certain way, a bone that broke and never set right. My hairdresser is from Nebraska. My boss is from Illinois. A friend from Kansas. People from Iowa, like me. I catch myself describing my hometown like it was a combat outpost: a hundred degrees, middle of nowhere, everyone counting the days till we could leave. *How did you make it through?* we seem to ask each other. Personally, I worked at a gas station. My friends bagged groceries and cooked pizzas. We each had had a job to do, then on weekends we got blackout drunk on bottom-shelf vodka mixed with fruit punch. We moved at night. We felt invincible. We preempted every secret by saying, *I'm drunk, so you know I'm telling the truth.* (The secret was always *I want to kiss you.*) (The opposite of homesickness is still homesickness.) (There are a lot of ways to feel ill toward a place or a time.) (The ill of feeling too removed, and longing to return.) (The ill of feeling not removed enough.)

The town where I live now is prosperous, so the born-and-raised locals get defensive. They made all this, and they made it to be *like this.* The best thing is to be *from* here. To have helped make it. If you're not from here, be from somewhere hard and unpopular. Be from a place where people listen to Trisha Yearwood and the houses have unfinished basements and in the summer tornadoes rip trees out of the earth and hurl them into the next county and in the winter blizzards bury your car but the superintendent doesn't cancel school. Be either from here or from a land of imaginary suffering. I was raised to be uncomfortable with comfort, to distrust it, which means I know a lot of people who talk about the weather because they like to discuss what steadily distresses them, followed by *Can't complain.*

When someone asks where I am from, I say, *Eastern Iowa, a small town south of Iowa City.*

I want to say the place I am from is childhood, how about you?

The place I am from is youth.

The place I am from is memory, where my brother's heroes always had the best nicknames. Hakeem Olajuwon was *Hakeem the Dream.* Clyde Drexler was *Clyde the Glide.* Walter Payton was *Sweetness.* I remember as boys *sweetness* was the highest possible compliment. An amazing dunk, a sports car: *O! Sweetness.* Better than *awesome* or *cool.* Sweetness. The force we appreciated bore a quality of tenderness—strength as a kind of harmony, the finding of a path amid turbulence.

I want to say the place I am from is the fountain on the town square.

From the sour chemical smell of the orange soap that cut through engine grease.

From the chime at the end of church that meant we were sent forth.

From inverting the front of my sweatshirt to form a basket if I had a lot of small things to carry.

From eighth grade study hall when a boy stood before the television and laughed at the images of New Yorkers running from smoke.

From our school mascot, the Demons, which never struck me as odd. That we had chosen the devil to represent us. The demon was male, orange, hyper-muscular, with two short horns, a black goatee, and often a trident. At basketball games our student section wore black T-shirts with the demon's picture. Sometimes the opposing team's student section would dress all in white. They would build white crosses and stand in our bleachers and lift up the crosses and chant *Demon killers!*

Once after a game, the same kid who laughed at the fleeing New Yorkers approached one of the white-clad boys, stole his cross, and smashed it against the ground. This was a confusing statement—the kid who smashed it was Catholic—but even some of the parents cheered him. Demons are a complicated image, and a more complicated self-image. You want to avoid suggesting that you, personally, are the devil, while piggybacking on the threat of fiery eternal power. The mood you want to achieve is one of *menace*—the intersection of serious fear and rambunctiousness.

We needed from demons this limited version of terror. An image that violated every spiritual thing we claimed to believe but without erasing the beliefs entirely. Horns helped identify the figure, though it was best to avoid hooves.

Recently, a coworker told me about his son's high school cross-country meet. It featured two races. During the first race a runner on the course disturbed a hornet's nest. The second race was mayhem. A chaos of hornets. Boys ran panicked into the woods, to the nearest creek, submerging themselves for an hour hoping to relieve the burns. Four ambulances came. Barely anyone finished the race. The place you are from is the place where you were first chased by hornets. The place where, upon being chased, you knew the quickest way to the water.

As if *from* denotes the landscape of one's greatest vulnerability.

From is a referent to the forming of identity that happens prior to the forming of independence.

I say the runner *disturbed* the nest, but *disturb* implies that the hornets were overreacting. What we know is that the boys were proportionately gigantic, powerful, in love with the act of stampeding, and careless at how their own nature might be cause for alarm.

I am from two acres of property surrounded by cornfields.

From thinking these fields were infinite.

From learning they were not.

From wondering, What could infinity mean, if not this?

The Problem
of Landing

. . . .

Joe Klein came to the Midwest from somewhere else to write about a political event in the Rock Valley College gymnasium in Rockford, Illinois, on a Saturday morning in September 2006. *Time* magazine sent him, not just to Illinois but to subsequent events in Iowa, and while the story for *Time* begins in the Midwest, in the gymnasium in Rockford, the story isn't really about the nuances of midwestern life. Klein, who arrived from New York, says nothing about the sort of town Rockford might be, its hardships, its character, its past or present. He tells us that local people, a lot of them, have showed up for a rally, on a weekend, but mostly the event is a way to begin the mise-en-scène, a jumping-off point for a profile about the man rallying them. We meet some of the attendees briefly. A white woman named Greta just finished a twelve-hour shift as a nurse. Greta is excited. Her enthusiasm is the main thing. Enthusiasm allows the story to transcend place, makes the event relevant for a national audience. Greta's enthusiasm might soon become yours. Mine. Ours. Greta is fully psyched to meet the man at the story's center, who is from the Midwest, from Illinois, as well as from Hawaii and Indonesia. *From*, after all, is complicated. The complication and the enthusiasm are connected. Klein writes that his subject has a "distinctive portfolio of talents," which means a broad portfolio, which means his subject is versatile, dexterous.

Klein compares the man to Colin Powell, Oprah, John McCain, and Bill Clinton. The story, which runs in October 2006 under the headline "Why Barack Obama Could Be the Next President," defies place in order to invoke raw possibility. The crowds in Illinois and Iowa are "giddy." They pulse with "awe and ecstasy." Then they are gone. The crowds go wild and then disappear. That's how it works in the Midwest: people who are sometimes overlooked respond intensely to a political moment, and their response serves only to further obliterate them.

I picked up a real physical copy of *Time* somewhere on the campus in Iowa City during my first semester at the University of Iowa in the fall of 2006. I saw Barack Obama's photo on the cover. I read about the enthusiasm, the awe and ecstasy, and thought to myself something along the lines of *Holy fucking shit*. In the article, Klein writes, "The question of when Obama—who has not yet served two years in the U.S. Senate—will run for President is omnipresent. That he will eventually run, and win, is assumed by almost everyone who comes to watch him speak." I wanted to watch him speak. Luckily, I lived in Iowa. A few weeks later, in November 2006, I stood in a crowd on the pedestrian mall downtown. I don't know how many people were there but one journalist later described the crowd as "enormous." It felt enormous. It felt electric. Obama's style spanned from funny to serious to thoughtful to offbeat to casual to decorous, and not just one thing at a time but many things at once. He had range, and moving within the range seemed effortless.

Technically, Obama was stumping for the governor's race, but no one cared about the governor. Technically, Obama wouldn't enter the presidential contest for three more months, but we knew. Less than two years later, I attended my first and only Iowa caucus. I sat in the band room of my hometown junior high school and wore a sticker with Obama's name. A friend took a photo of me waiting for the caucus to start. I'm chatting with an older white woman who is wearing a black coat, cream sweater, and matching cream scarf. It was cold that night. The almanac says two below and windy. I'm wearing a gray Hawkeyes sweatshirt. I'd driven through snow and slush from the house where I grew up. The caucus was planned during winter break so college students like me would attend in our hometowns, dispersing the culture of Iowa City throughout the state. The woman and I both have the Obama stickers. We sit in metal folding chairs in the part of the room where the clarinet players used to sit, one tier above the flutes, stage left. The woman looks serious, contemplative. I am not calm. My smile is huge. I'm overjoyed.

I'm Greta. And I'm excited when it happens: Obama wins our county, then our state, and so on.

Not just excited. I'm proud.

. . . .

I grew up in a Republican family. Traditionalism ruled. Reunions were held on Labor Day weekend at a park in Louisa County, Iowa, where representatives from each household took turns standing to report their family's accomplishments. A designated secretary recorded minutes. Children fidgeted at their family's picnic table. I remember once an uncle or cousin mentioned during his family report then president Bill Clinton. He pronounced *Clinton* sharply, like the name was a bladed weapon recently used against him. *Clintton*. Hearing the word, someone else shouted, *Flip flop!*

Someone else said it, too: *Flip flop!*

More people joined in: *Flip! Flop!*

Soon they were chanting: *Flip! Flop! Flip! Flop! Flip! Flop!*

The man who began the chant held up his hand and turned it over and back to visualize his concern, or as if to keep them synchronized, like he was directing them. The moment just emerged. It came from nowhere and it came from somewhere and we looked at it briefly and then it was gone. I realized the people around me held in common this thing I hadn't previously known. I was probably nine, sitting at a picnic table in an otherwise quiet park in a small town in Louisa County.

. . . .

Even before moving there for college, I knew about Iowa City. I knew about Iowa City because it had everything, including mini golf. My family drove thirty miles to Iowa City once a year for mini golf. We drove there to visit the mall on weekends. We drove there to eat at Godfather's Pizza, which served *dessert* pizza and had an *arcade*. We drove there to visit Waldenbooks and B. Dalton Books and then later Barnes & Noble. The driver's ed teacher made us drive to Iowa City for our final exam because Iowa City had traffic. In high school, my friends and I drove there for movies because our local one-screen theater showed only family movies. We drove there to see *Brokeback Mountain* and *Fahrenheit 9/11* and *Saw*. We drove there because our older friends had moved there for college and we still needed them to buy us rum and vodka. We drove there for dinner on prom night. We drove there for rock shows at Gabe's Oasis. I remember standing in line at the bottom of the narrow stairs the same week a fire had erupted in another small club across the country, killing a hundred people. It happened during a Great White performance, and my friend looked at the tiny passage into the room where the bands would play and joked to the kids around us, "So, who's here to see Great White?" Someone said, "Man, that's not cool," and I wished I'd been the person who said it.

Everything that didn't exist in my hometown existed in Iowa City. The place felt limitless, always in new ways. Soon after I moved there for college, the senator from Illinois spoke to us on the pedestrian mall. Marilynne Robinson planned to speak to us in the library of the Dey House, but such a big crowd poured into the room we had to walk, all of us and Marilynne Robinson, to a lecture hall in the science building so she could deliver her essay about beauty. Zadie Smith came to town, and so did John McPhee and Colson Whitehead and Eula Biss. Other people, mostly teachers, had to explain to me how important everything was. What to do. Who to see. Take this class with this writer. Go to this show. Go to this reading. I remember sitting in a circle of chairs outside and someone asked Eula Biss if we were allowed to use composite characters in nonfiction and she said to ask yourself why you need to simplify the difficulty. If four people were in the room and you want to condense them into three, who is the fourth person and why might they seem unimportant to you? Did they not matter in the moment, or do you not yet understand how they mattered? Are you listening for the story that happened or hewing toward the story you already decided to tell?

Eventually, I learned where the graduate students dropped off their stories and poems for workshop, in the cubbies in the Dey House basement, and I stole packets for myself to see the kind of art they were making. These people who had come to Iowa because it meant something important to them, something slightly different from what it had always meant to me. I learned that Iowa meant more than my hometown or Louisa County or anyplace in particular. Iowa meant a certain limitlessness, which in turn meant a beguiling, tenacious complexity. Which for some reason reminds me again of Biss, who seems to love writing toward moments that wreck her ability to understand. In an essay about pain she writes, "Euclid proved the number of primes to be infinite, but the infinity of primes is slightly smaller than the infinity of the rest of the numbers. It is here, exactly at this point, that my ability to comprehend begins to fail." To address the topic of pain, Biss spends one page thinking about the number seven, which is both simple and connected to limitlessness, a combination that exhausts her capacity for sensemaking. That is exactly how I feel about every aspect of the Midwest.

. . . .

The rhetorical situation of a transplant is complicated. I was born in Iowa, grew up there, attended college there, but I've lived on the West Coast for nine years now, mostly in Oregon. I spend a lot of time reading about the Midwest because I'm interested in the ways midwesterners represent themselves, how they must ferociously contend with stereotypes, how they must describe an experience of place while dislodging whatever mistaken idea of that place a reader might've anticipated. But reading about the Midwest is strange. I'm both an insider and an outsider. And what midwesterners tend to do with outsiders is talk down to them, as retaliation for being so routinely neglected and dismissed. I am presumed to be full of mistaken ideas, which often I am. I've been gone awhile, and I don't know the place as well as I used to know it, but I still lived there for an amount of time that presently constitutes the majority of my life, but I've also lived *here* now for a while, too, so I get defensive of this place just as easily. I'm always a few different readers at once. Probably so are you.

Lately I've been reading *The View from Flyover Country: Dispatches from the Forgotten America* by Sarah Kendzior and Meghan O'Gieblyn's *Interior States*, which includes her essay "Dispatch from Flyover Country." The writers seem to be addressing my sort of gaze. A *dispatch* from flyover country, from the forgotten America, is presumably sent beyond the region's borders, probably to correct a mistaken perspective. The authors are confronting a larger-than-usual gap between author and audience. In Sarah Smarsh's *Heartland*, a memoir about growing up poor in rural Kansas, the perspective is a little different. Smarsh writes to a hypothetical future daughter, August. The reader eavesdrops on lessons, instructions, stories, warnings. Smarsh explains to August, for example, "We were of a place, the Great Plains, spurned by more powerful corners of the country as a monolithic cultural wasteland. 'Flyover country,' people called it, like walking there might be dangerous. Its people were 'backward,' 'rednecks.' Maybe even 'trash.'" The memoir's form accuses while disarming the accusation. *People* called us these names. *People* dismissed us. Maybe the reader is one of those people and maybe not.

I feel drawn to the term "flyover country" because it's such an effective and grating dismissal. It holds place at an extreme distance. It denies granularity. The travelers are staying at 30,000 feet. If anything, they're looking out heavy windows at square fields, meandering rivers, cul-de-sacs. The phrase is formed out of both neglect and attention, or maybe the strange intersection of neglect and attention. "Flyover country" points at a place for the purpose of dismissing it, but the term seems to be invoked most often by people reasserting that place, reclaiming its significance, dislodging a stereotype. The Midwest is named in order to make it vanish in order to make it reappear.

The Midwest must make itself reappear constantly. In *The View from Flyover Country*, Kendzior writes, "The Midwest, in decline for decades, still suffers disproportionately. We get attention when there's a murder, a protest, an election. Otherwise, we are treated as pawns in a media-staged hunger games, as parachute journalists swoop in for riots and rallies, as people who would never deign to live in a place like my city tell the world what it truly represents, who we truly are." The reader of journalism can't understand the riots or rallies or elections unless they understand what happens between those events, what sort of community hosts them. Kendzior's work addresses that narrative disparity—not telling the "real story" of an election but the story that was never given the chance to be misunderstood.

It's delicate. To establish a place's identity in the mind of someone who doesn't live there. The events Kendzior mentions—riots, protests, rallies, murders, elections—are what I might describe as *the news*. Maybe it's forgivable, even ordinary, that the Midwest "gets attention" only when news happens there. In 2020, Oregon made the national news for its protests, its rallies, what some called its riots, and its historically destructive fire season. The state got attention for its most visibly extreme behaviors. Four years earlier, eastern Oregon got national attention when armed men took over the Malheur National Wildlife Refuge. Some readers of that news were probably reading about eastern Oregon—a rural geography about the size of Iowa—for the first time. People who would never deign to live there arrived to tell the world what it truly represents. Eastern Oregon is another place more often flown over than visited. What interests me is how both acts are a problem. *Flyover country* is a wound of inattention rarely healed by attention. A wound that sometimes worsens when a person descends, visits, decides to look around. There is the problem of flying over but there is also the problem of landing.

Louisa County, where my family gathers for reunions, also made the national news in 2020, when its largest employer, the Tyson meatpacking plant, sustained a coronavirus outbreak that infected 522 of its 1,300 workers, most of whom are Latino. Two of the workers died. Tyson stayed in the news throughout the year: lawsuits, filed against another of the company's meatpacking plants in northern Iowa, accused managers of betting on how many of the workers would get infected, forcing employees to continue working after testing positive for the virus, and lying to interpreters about the health risks of working in a crowded space during a pandemic. I don't know whether the coverage fairly represented the place or if someone who never deigned to live there misconstrued what the place truly represents. I don't know what the place truly represents. I know my family's annual reunion went on during the pandemic. People gathered. They shared food. They declined masks. I didn't go. The invitation pissed me off, but I kept the anger to myself, per the tradition.

. . . .

By the 2012 election I had moved to California. I worked for an e-commerce start-up in San Francisco's Financial District, where many of my coworkers were born-and-raised Californians. Marta commuted from Oakland, where she and her wife had recently bought a home. Marta played drums in a punk band that lacked a guitarist, but somehow they made it work for them. I admired how Marta was settling down; she had a mortgage now, but she also had the band. She could be both people.

Marta balked at Iowa's role in the election. I forget how the topic came up. There wasn't a meaningful Democratic caucus in 2012—the Iowa caucus wouldn't have been important news—but I remember she scoffed at Iowa being first in the primary season. That a bunch of farmers and rural white people should set the pace for the nation. I tried to explain that Iowa was more than one thing. More than its stereotypes. I felt confident in making this point because I'd recently watched a YouTube video that argued the same thing. I'd found the video persuasive. It was called "Iowa Nice" and I told Marta to look it up.

The video is less than two minutes long, and in the last nine years it has received more than 1.5 million views. It begins with a man speaking to the camera. The man is white, bearded, in his late twenties, and wearing thick-framed glasses. In the background are satellite trucks, one of which belongs to CNN, no doubt in town for the election cycle. "So I hear you

The Problem of Landing

know something about Iowa?" says the speaker. "Fuck you." The speaker is local actor Scott Siepker, and he is here to offer a defense of Iowa and its politics. The defense has two prongs: Iowa is more liberal than you think (the state was one of the first to legalize gay marriage), and the part of the state you interpret as conservative is actually more intellectual than you think, a logic apparently meant to rescue conservative Iowans from their conservatism. Scott says about farming, "It takes a fleet of tricked-out machines and a shit-ton of ag science to make it all work." Not only are farmers smart, they're *cool*. They drive *tricked-out machines*. He adds that most Iowans live in cities, which is technically true provided your definition of *city* is generous enough to include any place in Iowa. The population densities of Des Moines and Iowa City are roughly a third the density of Minneapolis and a quarter the density of Chicago. Two square miles of Manhattan outnumber all seventy square miles of Cedar Rapids. In short, I now believe he's reaching.

I'm curious what he's reaching *for*. At first, the video's purpose seems to be challenging as many stereotypes as possible. Farming isn't just dragging around a plow; farming is complicated, expensive, and technological. Iowa's politics aren't close-minded or regressive; the first female lawyer in America received her degree in Iowa City. And the character of Iowa isn't just *nice*; the speaker looks at the camera, at us, and swears at us a bunch of times. But the purpose of the video isn't counterargument. The purpose is counter-contempt. The speaker *doesn't like you either*. Scott looks bored. His eyes never fully open. He never appears intense or excited, because he is annoyed, because you are annoying. Your ignorance is exhausting, and Iowans are tired of being nice about it.

As a recent transplant to California, suddenly surrounded by people who didn't know much about Iowa, I loved watching this video. I loved how Iowa could be smart and tough and generous and hard-working and sneering and nice, all at the same time. "Next time you fly over? Give us a wave," says Scott. "We'll wave back. We're nice. That's right. We're nice. Fuckwad."

The contempt seems, now, a little adolescent. It's based more on perception than reality—the speaker stereotyping the people stereotyping him. He expects, for example, that his presumably coastal audience doesn't know much about agriculture. Smarsh takes a similar position in *Heartland*: "For someone who never worked a farm, for whom the bread and meat in deli sandwiches seemed to magically materialize without agricultural labor, the center of the country was a place flown over but not touched." Notice how the sentence doesn't distinguish between farmers and non-farmers but between non-farmers and "the center of the country." In this view, people who live in the center know about farming, and people who live on the coasts believe food arrives in stores by *magic*. This thinking ignores the state of California, America's leading grower of vegetables. It ignores Washington state, the country's leading grower of apples. It ignores the entire West Coast, which produces 94 percent of the country's wine. Plenty of people on both coasts know how to harvest.

The discourse on flyover country often deploys one stereotype for the purpose of dispelling another. The person we invent to misunderstand us rarely benefits from the pain we feel at being misunderstood. Smarsh, for instance, insists her region is either ignored or treated with clichés: "I rarely saw the place I called home described or tended to in political discourse, the news media, or popular culture as anything but a stereotype or something that happened a hundred years ago." Then later: "I saw many white girls on television, but I rarely recognized myself in their stories. When I did see my place or people, they were usually represented as caricatures." But feeling misrepresented hasn't compelled Smarsh to see people from different parts of the country with a more generous lens. Her representation of a city person is parody: "When affluent urban men in plaid flannel shirts let their hair grow wild and unkempt across their face and necks to affect a laborer's style for doing laptop work in coffee shops, I think of my dad immaculately trimming his beard every morning before dawn to work on a construction site." The representation of urban versus rural is trite on both counts. Rich hipsters on laptops in coffee shops, so embarrassed by their failure to perform physical labor that they imitate an image of it. Meanwhile, the true, disciplined worker rises every morning before dawn. That a man with unkempt hair working in a coffee shop somehow signals "affluent" is a little suspicious. At the very least, the affluence isn't self-evident. People who work in coffee shops are likely to be stringing together part-time jobs, undergoing economic stress, but they're not described in terms of their potential hardship, nor in terms of personal discipline. We don't know what time the "urban man" set his alarm. We only know he is a poseur.

It's a small point. Especially compared with the excellent work Smarsh does outlining cycles of generational poverty and violence. Her study of the Midwest is incredibly insightful. But it's grating to me how she presumes her audience to be so cartoonishly misinformed, how the story partly fabricates the distance it means to close.

. . . .

In the spring of 2008, the semester after I caucused for Obama, I took a class called Anthropology and Contemporary World Problems. The professor assigned Deborah Fink's 1998 ethnography *Cutting into the Meatpacking Line: Workers and Change in the Rural Midwest,* in which Fink goes to work at a meatpacking plant in Perry, Iowa, for five months and interviews more than a hundred people. She describes extremely hazardous working conditions, cruel management, rampant sexism, a system built to exploit wage labor. She calls the conditions "evil." She calls the experience "physical and emotional carnage." I didn't like the book. I didn't like Deborah, and I didn't like my professor for assigning it. It seemed to me like the author had showed up to a dangerous workplace, learned it was dangerous, and complained about the danger. What did she expect. What did she think went on in a place like that. Who didn't know that already.

Me, for one. I didn't know that already. The book showed me these brutal conditions for the first time, and I immediately found reasons to defend them. I read about exploitation and justified it to myself in ways that made me feel better. People chose to work there. They could work somewhere else if they wanted. Deborah could leave anytime, if she wanted. Don't eat pork, if it upsets you so much. That's a choice you have. Most things struck me as choices. I didn't consider whether my reaction might've been different if the author had been a man, or if the professor who assigned it had been a man, or if the conditions had occurred not in rural Iowa but in South Dakota or Peru. I didn't like Fink paying so much attention to rural Iowa, and I didn't like what she saw there. The conditions seemed like her fault because she had seen them.

Part of Fink's goal in *Cutting into the Meatpacking Line* is to subvert popular understandings of agricultural labor in the Midwest. How farming is often seen through a romanticized lens—an independent family's diligent production of goods for their community. An idealism of American effort. In the "Iowa Nice" video, the speaker boasts, "One Iowa farmer feeds 155 of you." But that's not how it works. Fink reminds us that one farmer doesn't feed anyone alone. Raising livestock means slaughtering livestock and packaging it, which means an enormous industry of exploitative labor.

The romantic notion is a mirage designed to blur conflicts of class and power. The romantic notion requires inattention to exist.

. . . .

My work friend Marta watched the Iowa video. She wasn't convinced. Maybe for the same reasons I can't stomach it now. Maybe the speaker chooses unconvincing examples. Maybe in complicating the stereotype he still chooses to elide complication. How does the assertion of "Iowa nice" intersect with its whiteness? How does his claim about Iowa's liberal politics—"We went Democratic in five out of the last six presidential elections"—change now that the statistic has shifted: Iowa has gone Democratic in five of the last eight? And what happens when the state's liberalism is overridden by its conservatism? During the coronavirus pandemic, Iowa's Republican governor declined to implement any meaningful measures to prevent the spread of the virus, claiming such measures would violate Iowans' personal freedoms. Accordingly, deaths per capita in Iowa tripled the rate here in Oregon, where the liberal governor instituted mandates on masks, physical distancing, and business operations. If Iowa had mitigated the virus to the same extent Oregon did, hundreds of Iowans might still be alive.

The video has a certain swagger, an arrogance that might feel charming if it was deployed on your behalf. When the speaker boasts about the last six presidential elections, he holds up a cardboard cutout of Barack Obama's smiling face and says, "How do you like me now?"

I've felt that pride, too.

. . . .

Sometimes it's joyful to learn all over again about the place you're from, and sometimes it isn't. How Iowa awarded its electoral votes in 2016 surprised me. Maybe I shouldn't have been surprised, but I was. Maybe I should've known better, but I didn't. I had questions. What just happened? Why did it happen? How do we prevent it from happening again? Who exactly is "we"? Such questions were common after the election and soon became cliché, but the questions persist for me, and I appreciate the way Claudia Rankine raises them in her 2020 book *Just Us: An American Conversation*. She describes the "built-in violence of white supremacy" that characterized the Trump administration and says, "Those who voted in 2016 to be represented yet again by this form of violence, the 62 percent of white men and 47 percent of white women, a plurality, how am I to understand them? How should I understand their origin stories?" Later, she poses the question this way: "Why aren't all people actively involved in our present American struggle against a nationalist regime?" After the 2016 election, journalists traveled to the rural Midwest to raise similar questions. They wanted to locate members of the plurality. They wanted to have a conversation. Why aren't you involved in the present American struggle against a nationalist regime? How are people to understand you? How should anyone understand your origin story?

Many reporters who raised these questions failed to raise them well, and their project has since been rightfully skewered. The stories were excessively narrow, focusing on voters who supported Obama in 2012 and then Trump in 2016. Iowa had a high percentage of these voters, and because Iowa is disproportionately white and because Trump voters were disproportionately white and male and old, the post-2016 story centered on a hyper-specific kind of American, viewed through a flawed lens. Here is Trip Gabriel writing for the *New York Times* in January 2017: "Jones County [Iowa], which includes Monticello, is the birthplace of the painter Grant Wood, and where older men still wear the style of pinstriped overalls in his 'American Gothic.' It is a beautiful place, with bald eagles soaring over wintry farm fields. Mr. Trump carried the county by 20 percentage points; Mr. Obama easily won there four years earlier."

This passage comes from a story about seven older white men who gather each morning at a diner to talk politics. It's true, I want to know what these men are talking about. I want to know what they're thinking, and I appreciate that someone asked, but I wish someone *else* had asked, or I wish their responses had been allowed a more nuanced context. Gabriel can't help but figure these men as almost sickeningly American. For instance, it would've been possible to describe the Iowa landscape without choosing to name the very symbolic bald eagle. It would've been possible to describe the men's clothing without invoking *American Gothic*, a painting the men probably don't give a shit about, a painting that reveals more about the writer's perspective than the subjects' lived context. Even complimenting Iowa as *beautiful* seems to betray an assumption that it might've been otherwise, as if Gabriel was surprised to find that a place could be so aesthetically wonderful in spite of its endorsement of the nationalist regime.

I think it's important to understand what happened in Jones County, but the pursuit of understanding was overly generous, indulgent, framed in a nostalgia similar to the one that saturated the nationalist regime's campaign. In other words, I'm worried about the nostalgia of the people who voted to *Make America Great Again*, but I'm also worried about the nostalgia of Trip Gabriel, the man who landed in Iowa and decided to look around. Part of my concern is that Gabriel's rendering of eastern Iowa is technically accurate. Jones County is the birthplace of Grant Wood. Some men who live there really wear a certain style of overalls. America's national bird flies overhead. And yet: Bald eagles have an enormous range across North America. Their existence in eastern Iowa is not unique to eastern Iowa. They can be found, depending on the season, throughout most of the country. But Trip Gabriel decided to point them out here. In the beautiful place. *Soaring over wintry farm fields.*

I'm worried about the difficulty of seeing a place and knowing it. How the problem of flying over so easily gives way to the problem of landing. Everything Gabriel saw was there. Everything he didn't see was there too. The questions he asked were necessary, but they weren't the only necessary questions. In a 2018 essay, Tamara Winfrey-Harris writes, "The so-called flyover states have long been an avatar for the real America—small towns, country music, conservatism, casseroles and amber waves of grain. Whiteness. It is that mythologized heartland that pundits seem to think will engender empathy, not the Black families of Milwaukee; the majority-Latino community of Dodge City, Kansas; the Burmese Chin refugees of Indianapolis; or the strong Arab community of metropolitan Detroit."

This idea, too, is strung with tension: *The so-called flyover states have long been an avatar for the real America.* The tension is between irrelevance and centrality. The place known as *flyover country*, the place not worth seeing or understanding, is also the place too many people use to define America. Somehow the Midwest is both a land of obscurity and a paradigm of the American real. The two ideas are made from each other. The romantic notion requires inattention to exist.

It also requires a practiced quietism, a guardedness. It requires a skill for concealment. Trip Gabriel saw what he saw because of his own biases, but he also saw what he was allowed to see. Midwestern people know how to do their own public relations. They know how to protect their image. In 2006, the people who thrilled to see Barack Obama speak in the gymnasium in Rockford were described for their enthusiasm. Those people spoke to *Time.* The people who resented the senator's ascendance spoke, instead, to each other.

. . . .

I fly over Iowa sometimes. Most of the time I fly over Iowa because I'm actually trying to land there, and arriving in Iowa is never straightforward.

My flight from Oregon usually connects through Chicago, so I have to fly east, overshoot the place I'm going, change planes, fly back west to Des Moines, then drive back east to my hometown, which is in between Chicago and Des Moines. Getting there is ridiculous, so when I finally arrive into the living room of the house where I grew up and my parents ask how was the flight, I like to remind them there were two flights and two drives. I take them all the way through it so they understand I went to great lengths to be here. I make crossing the country seem both arduous and plain. I describe two events that happened during the trip, then say the trip was uneventful. If snow almost carried my rental car off the highway, I tell them the roads aren't great. If my arms are sore from white-knuckling the steering wheel through wind and ice, I tell them the roads are bad but I took it easy and it was fine.

Probably my favorite essay about the Midwest is Meghan O'Gieblyn's "Dispatch from Flyover Country," in which the region is permitted its fuller kaleidoscopic strangeness. It is at once Chicago and Madison and the western shores of Michigan, at once pastoral, gentrified, industrial, thriving, surreal, faithful, secular, polite, bitter, skeptical, and extremely cold in winter. O'Gieblyn describes and performs a local temperament, what it can mean to live there or be from there or both, a sensibility that never tries to outmaneuver its own perpetual contradiction. Every simplicity is beset by history, politics, money. Every statement about the region's meaning strikes me as exactly correct and impossible. Not wrong, but impossible. A kind of impossibility that feels to me extremely midwestern.

In one scene, friends have returned from San Francisco to rural Michigan and over dinner evangelize about their shiny lives in the tech industry. True to form, the costal people are obnoxious snobs, fatally in love with their own success. I deeply enjoy O'Gieblyn's disdain for the tech people, because I've met those people and felt that disdain too. She jabs at the way they've succumbed to euphemistic corporate utopianism and offers that such thinking wouldn't last long in the Midwest: "Here, work is work and money is money, and nobody speaks of these things as though they were spiritual movements or expressions of one's identity." This is both true and something else. I appreciate the tautological assertion that a simple word has a simple meaning. Work is work. Is work. Is work. I appreciate the recognition that not everyone wants to think about their shitty wage job as a vehicle for realizing an idealistic moral philosophy. But this ethic toward work and money doesn't change the importance of work and money. Nobody speaks of these things as expressions of identity, and yet they are expressions of identity. *Hard-working* is possibly the region's profoundest compliment. I would go so far as to call the midwestern obsession with work and productivity a spiritual movement, even if the movement doesn't announce itself with the same coastal hubris. To say that *work is work* is an insistence on not saying more, rounding the sentence back on itself to avoid an idea rather than articulate one. It's plainness as a rhetorical tactic. Silence as an argument. Rooted in the statement is a further admission to midwestern character insofar as such a thing can exist: *Nobody speaks of these things.*

Central Crossings

. . . .

Fred Elm always told the same stories to every new batch of student employees. Fred had been a manager at the university bookstore for a long time.
He spoke gently. He smiled. He had gray hair. He liked surrealism. One of
the stories Fred Elm told over and over was about his friend, a painter, who
once painted a warehouse scene that Fred adored: in the painting, a forklift
was raising a pallet to place it among a lot of other pallets, and you had to
look close—you had to glance again—you had to refocus—to realize that
what sat on the pallet being hoisted by the forklift was not a stack of boxes
but a huge porcelain coffee cup on a huge porcelain saucer.

Steam rose from the cup.

But it took a moment to see that.

First the scene looked ordinary—boring—but then the boredom got
overturned by the ridiculous.

Or not the ridiculous, but a different kind of seriousness.

Suddenly the warehouse was a site of delicacy.

Suddenly the forklift driver was taking great care not to spill the coffee.

The way Fred Elm explained his admiration for the warehouse-coffee-
cup painting, you got the sense he felt the painting's weirdness required a
certain bravery. Like the painting was a very steep bet.

You got the sense he had this bravery within himself only on occasion.

I liked Fred.

Fred never fired anyone even when they probably deserved it. He gave everyone a lot of chances. He let the store be slightly inefficient due to a surplus of errors. He knew exactly how much leeway he had and disbursed the leeway generously. His generosity seemed to imply a belief that the work would get done no matter what. That the books would always get to the people who needed them. His manner seemed to presuppose that the world was indestructible. It's possible I'm projecting. But that's how the world seemed to seem to Fred Elm.

He explained where to stack the books and where to shelve them.

He had a system.

The work always got done.

Batch after batch of students arrived and he showed them how to do a bookstore.

. . . .

I had been working in the bookstore for one year when the store was destroyed in a flood. The bookstore was in the basement of the Iowa Memorial Union, which sat beside the Iowa River, which bisected the campus in Iowa City. In the summer of 2008 the river exceeded its banks by nine feet and flooded twenty buildings on campus and nearly a hundred homes.

The river went inside the Memorial Union.

The river went inside the National Guard armory and the water treatment plant.

The river was on top of the interstate.

The river was on top of First Avenue in the next town over.

The river was in places that were usually nowhere near the river.

Engineers drilled holes in the pedestrian bridges so the river would flow through the holes instead of tearing the bridges off their foundations, which had happened in other towns.

The pedestrian bridges were saved.

The armory and the water treatment plant were not.

Both got demolished.

The present we had been living in got demolished.

The present got demolished not just by a new, updated edition of the present but by the future.

The future came in hard. The future arrived with some real enthusiasm.

. . . .

When something like this happens, you have to get creative.

The art building was destroyed, so art classes were moved to a former hardware store.

The auditorium was destroyed, so the ballet performed at theaters in Chicago and Des Moines.

The orchestra performed at a casino conference room.

The magician performed at a local high school.

The brass band performed on the campus lawn.

The bookstore was destroyed, so our books were moved into the Old Capitol Mall, uphill from the river, into a space recently vacated by a consignment shop. Fred instructed us to stack boxes of textbooks in the dressing rooms, but there were not nearly enough dressing rooms, so warehouse space was procured at a building on South Gilbert Street, a building the university owned as a distribution center for apparel, supplying shirts to the football stadium. Fred dispatched five of his most experienced students to be a team at the warehouse. The people who already worked there made room in the refrigerator for our lunches. I remember Michelle, who had worked for the bookstore longer than me, assessing our new space. The forklifts. The incredible heat. The isolation. Pickers climbed ladders, grabbing plastic-wrapped shirts from plastic buckets, fulfilling internet orders. Almost everyone listened to headphones. Except Linda. Linda, who managed receiving and who had worked in the warehouse for many years, was cheerful almost all the time and wanted to talk to everyone to tell them how they were doing such a great job.

Michelle was thoughtful, articulate, friendly, and I remember she said this about Linda:

You would have to have a good attitude to work in a place like this.

Like the place would drain you.

Like the sadness was inevitable.

Like the joy was nothing but a learned barrier, an emergency response to the environment.

I tried to have a good attitude. I liked the work sometimes. Lifting the boxes, driving the pallets around, it was physical work, and physical work made me feel useful, like a horse. And it was physical work in service of intellectual work. The books were about physics, business, microbiology, macroeconomics. Intro to Literature was teaching *The Handmaid's Tale*, *Autobiography of Red*, and an anthology of short stories with James Baldwin, Sandra Cisneros, Flannery O'Connor, and Gabriel García Márquez. I liked the weight of the books. The space they took up. Trucks backed against the loading dock so we could scoot pallet jacks between the wooden slats and haul the work of Anne Carson into a huge room where it waited for its trip to the store, where at least one student would take it from the shelf, carry it to their dorm, open it up, start to read, and think, Wait, you can do that? You're allowed to *do that?*

You are.

You are allowed to do that.

In fact, you have to.

You have to puncture the bridges to make way for the water.

You have to place a coffee cup where, at first, it does not seem to belong.

You have to come at it with a little creativity.

You have to have a good attitude to work in a place like this.

You have to get used to it.

You will have to spend a lot of time in places like this.

Most places, in fact, will turn out to be *like this.*

．．

I was living in Iowa City again. I had graduated from the university, then spent an intervening year in Afghanistan. My fiancée Jessica and I rented a studio apartment on South Clinton Street, one block from the county court-house, with its two looming sandstone turrets, and one block diagonally from the post office, where Jessica had mailed letters to me during the time I was gone. The apartment had a bright red bathroom floor. Our mattress lay in the corner of the main room. The porch had a porch swing where we sat and drank coffee and planned our wedding, which would take place at a hotel four blocks north, downtown, followed by a honeymoon on a Croatian island in the Adriatic Sea, followed by our plan to move to California. We felt we didn't belong in Iowa City anymore.

In the meantime I needed work, so I brought my résumé to a temp agency.

They paid me to serve pizza at a biotechnology research conference.

They paid me to serve barbecue pork at a wedding reception at the Old Brick Church.

They paid me to answer phones for a construction contractor, which was bidding on the renovation of a sports arena in Cedar Rapids. The arena had been damaged in the flood three years earlier. The renovation would require subcontractors for plumbing, electrical, and flooring and a special firm to rebuild the escalators, all of whom faxed in their estimates the day the bid was due. I checked the fax machine every five minutes, but Mark, the project manager, said that wasn't often enough, I want you to stand *right here* in front of the machine and tell me as *soon* as an estimate arrives. So I was paid to stand *right here* in front of the fax machine and as *soon* as an estimate arrived, I hurried the paper over to Mark's corner office so he could assemble the company's bid, which was rejected.

I was paid to answer phones for the planning department at city hall, while the regular secretary was on leave receiving cancer treatments. I answered a call from a woman who wanted to know if the city had dispensed a white panel van to her block. The van had been parked outside her home every day for a week. I asked around the office and learned the van did not belong to the City of Iowa City and offered to transfer her call to the police department.

I scanned documents. Faxed documents. I brewed coffee.

I loved brewing coffee.

When I first came home, I had taken my résumé to every coffee shop in Iowa City. Overseas, I had brewed coffee for my platoon. I loved sharing coffee with people. I loved drinking chai with the Afghan interpreters and security guards. How you could stop in the middle of anything and become closer to people if you had a hot enough beverage. But no shops in Iowa City would let me brew their coffee. So I made it for the planning department.

People love to arrive somewhere and be told the coffee is on.

They say, *Ohthankgod.*

They act like they have been searching all night for a hospital.

They act like they have been holding their breath underwater and just pierced the surface.

They act like what you have done is a miracle.

So I made coffee. I answered phones. I read the city's planning documents. Here is what I learned: after the flood, the city had invited "key stakeholders" to do interviews about the future of the neighborhoods affected by the flood, including the neighborhood where I now lived, between downtown and the river.

The stakeholders had been invited to do "visioning."

The stakeholders had been invited to do a SWOT analysis: Strengths, Weaknesses, Opportunities, Threats.

A strength was "proximity to the University of Iowa."

A threat was "drunken bar patrons."

A strength was "the Iowa River."

A threat was "flooding."

A weakness was "homeless population nearby."

A threat was "new low-income housing."

I learned the street outside my apartment would be widened into a "promenade" to better connect downtown with the new parks being built in the floodplain. A light rail stop would be constructed along the current tracks, dispensing passengers who would spend money at the new small businesses, described as "local flair—'mom and pop' stores." I learned my neighborhood was called Central Crossings, because people would be crossing through to reach the new beautiful spaces being made on the land the river had ruined.

. . . .

For a month I worked in an auto parts factory just off Highway 1, a building I had driven past but never really seen. The factory molded plastic into dashboards and interior paneling. It had a shop where machinists checked out parts and tools to repair their equipment. Nothing in the tool shop had been inventoried in forty years, so a man whose name I've forgotten was contracted to do so, but the job was so big he subcontracted the work by calling the temp agency. I counted gaskets and spark plugs. Most of the parts were upstairs in the shop's attic, walled in by chain-link fence and thus overlooking the factory floor. Shelves held motors the size of microwaves. The man in charge told me to make a pile of anything that looked broken and make a count of everything else.

I had no idea what was broken, so the man had to review the pile. Sometimes he would remove a motor and say, This is in fine condition and it costs $10,000. Let's keep it.

Like we were deciding together.

I'd say, Yeah, let's keep it.

I organized the drill bits. I kept my counts on a clipboard. Grease stained the papers. Grease stained my jeans and T-shirt, stained through my shoes to my socks, through my socks to my toenails. My skin smelled like motor oil. I ate lunch in my car in the parking lot because the machinists intimidated me; the break room was loud and crowded and they would know I wasn't one of them. I didn't own steel-toed footwear. I didn't know to bring my own earplugs and protective glasses to wear on the factory floor, so the supervisor had to lend them to me. On the floor, yellow lines marked where you could walk. Forklifts beeped around corners. Signs hanging from the rafters announced what vehicles the parts were being made for.

Jeep Patriot.

Chevrolet Corvette.

The factory wanted you to imagine the end result.

The factory wanted you to keep your eye on the ball.

Remember what you're a part of.

Some person in the future will be cruising the Pacific Coast Highway and you will have been the builder of their ecstasy, which means the ecstasy belongs, in part, to you.

It belongs to you in advance.

It belongs to you right now.

Try to feel it.

. . . .

When I headed back to the apartment, the only parking spaces in the neighborhood were on the other side of the tracks, and often a train was parked on the tracks because our street was not yet a promenade, so I had to climb over a hitch between the cars. The grease of the hitch didn't bother me because I was already like this.

. . . .

Jessica was paid to supervise the night shift at a shelter for kids who couldn't live at home. The kids had gotten in trouble with law enforcement, or the parents had, or the kids were transitioning from state-run care facilities to foster families. The shelter was south of the highway, on a side street, behind the grocery store. Even if you've lived in Iowa City your whole life you've probably never seen it.

Places like this are hard to find.

The most important thing is that they are not in your backyard.

Space that is no one's backyard is usually no one's backyard for a reason.

Another word for space that is no one's backyard is *floodplain*.

. . . .

Jessica and I moved to San Francisco. We piled our things into the Taurus, which sagged from the density of our belongings, which made me feel sure we would break down in Utah or Nevada, but we drove and drove, and slept, and arrived, and lived at a hotel near the airport for five days before moving into a two-bedroom flat two blocks from Golden Gate Park—the forest I soon learned was built on a sand dune—and eight blocks from Ocean Beach, which I soon learned usually had a bulldozer crawling over it, shoving the sand back into place, trying to prevent the beach's erosion into the sea.

If you think a job is temporary, consider a beach.

If you think a beach is temporary, consider an auditorium.

Consider an arena.

Compare the future with the present it demolishes.

Compare what we thought the climate could obliterate with what the climate, in fact, can obliterate.

Compare the National Guard armory, which still had horse stables on its lower level from the time it housed a cavalry unit, with the grassy park that was built on the same lot after the building was destroyed.

The first time I walked to the beach, a bulldozer was tracking across the sand, trying to impose *beach* onto the continent's edge.

I'm just saying what you arrive to is already a frailty.

I'm just saying who you become is a frailty.

I'm just saying things are going to break.

I'm saying they are breaking.

I'm saying you better be ready to respond.

You better be ready to do something.

In California, we lived with another couple. David was a developer working on an app that scraped songs from YouTube and imported them into a music player, for some reason. He was a DJ on the side. Olivia was an opera singer, with a rock band on the side.

Olivia's voice was magnificent.

Its power felt elegant, like the power of a star exploding.

She wanted to make it.

She was getting there.

She had gotten a callback from *The Voice* and now spent her afternoons rehearsing the song she would perform, a cover of Radiohead's "Creep."

Olivia's voice was beautiful in a way that Thom Yorke's voice was not— grander, and the grandness she gave the song made it more haunting. I overheard her sing this version of "Creep" maybe thirty times. She was hurt when the show rejected her. She knew it was silly and commercial, but she had wanted it. She had dressed up for the performance. She owned a lot of elaborate costumes, with sequins and feathers. She knew you had to *make* the cameras look at you. She had *arrived* at the auditorium. People had noticed. They had *looked*. Olivia understood their looking mattered as much as the music.

Olivia introduced herself to us as an opera singer, but she didn't perform with a company or perform in public very often. For money, Olivia taught voice lessons on a piano in the living room. The piano is why Olivia and David had agreed to live in the flat. The piano belonged to the landlord, who once lived in the same space and, upon leaving, hadn't wanted to move it. Once, Olivia wanted to make a music video, so she dragged the piano to the center of the living room and performed one of her band's songs while David filmed her. She sat sideways to the piano, corkscrewing her upper torso to the keys. Later she explained this was a very difficult posture to hold for the length of the song, and indeed it looked forced and awkward and made me wonder why she wasn't sitting at the piano the right way. But that was the idea. You were supposed to notice. The posture demonstrated her strength. That's what the song was about.

. . . .

I wanted a job at Starbucks so I could brew coffee, but it took them two months to call me back and by then I had gotten an office job in the Financial District. I worked for a start-up, though technically I worked for a staffing agency, which contracted me into the office where I worked.

Because I was not technically an employee of the company, I was ineligible for benefits.

Most employees of the company were not technically employees of the company.

I received minimum wage. I rode a bus from the city's oceanside to its downtown, which smelled like cappuccino and piss and bread being made. My office was on the seventh floor of the Shell Building, which stood on the last block of the city's real ground. A line etched in the sidewalk showed where the true earth stopped and the landfill began—where in the nineteenth century ships abandoned by gold miners were sunk in place, buried, and covered with asphalt and concrete to create room for more city. To impose *city* onto the water.

The company where I worked didn't require a special skill set, so it attracted artist types.

Marta drummed in a band.

Rebecca cartooned.

Andrew played jazz.

Celeste modeled.

Julie studied poetry at a graduate program.

Tyler was the ringleader of a steampunk-inspired alternative circus that performed at a warehouse in Oakland.

It was important to have something else going on.

Your something else made the office more tolerable and made you a more interesting person.

You're here, but who are you really?

You had to provide an identity that would overturn the fact that you worked in an office.

We rooted for each other's identities. We showed up.

We saw Marta's band play at Bottom of the Hill.

We went to Rebecca's art show, where they served craft beer and made-to-order pancakes.

We went to Tyler's circus and afterward got drunk with the fire-eaters while two trapeze artists dangled upside down from silk curtains in the middle of the room, making out with each other.

Of the kissing, Tyler seemed proud, like the quirkiness of the PDA was an expression of his own personality.

· ·

David and Olivia argued. We heard them. Their bedroom was supposed to be the flat's dining room, but it was advertised as a bedroom to increase the rent. The room had one door into the hall and one door into the kitchen, and David sealed off the door into the kitchen by stuffing the top and bottom with towels, but it didn't matter; the room lay in the center of the flat. It had been planned as a space to gather.

I'm just saying we heard them.

He threw things at her.

He screamed.

Objects shattered against the wall.

I didn't intervene.

Neither Jessica nor I knew what to do with them.

From the beginning, they seemed to believe we were simple, adorable midwesterners. Like our presence in the world was anachronistic. David and Olivia were not from the Midwest. She was from Portland. He was from Beirut. The Midwest astonished them. We did not own *any* elaborate costumes. We had nothing outlandish to wear to festivals or parades, and sometimes chose not even to attend festivals and parades. We didn't listen to Skrillex. Once, I was hand-washing a dish in the sink and David asked if I knew we had a dishwasher.

I told him I'd noticed it.

He told me hand-washing wastes water.

I said okay.

He said it really does.

He pointed at the dishwasher and said, Do you know what centrifugal force is?

We were people who probably hadn't heard about centrifugal force.

We were people who probably would've sat at the piano facing forward.

We would've worn slacks to the audition.

We would've sung "Creep" exactly as Yorke had done.

We had different sorts of lives.

Their shit was their shit, or so I had convinced myself.

When people tell you who they are, you are supposed to do something.

When the present demolishes the present, you are supposed to respond.

. . . .

On the seventh floor of the Shell Building, the company's engineers—all rock climbing enthusiasts—took a break every day at 2:00 P.M. to do push-ups in the conference room. Tyler joined them. Doing push-ups in the conference room thrilled Tyler. When the engineers walked over from the engineering side to the operations side, he glowed. It was a way of having something else going on. It was a hedge. You had to protect yourself from the possibility that what you were being paid to do amounted to an identity.

Andrew, the jazz player, grew up in Ohio and had come to San Francisco from graduate school in New Jersey, where he studied jazz performance. Andrew was a tall, skinny white guy with bony cheeks. His joints seemed to protrude because his limbs were so narrow. He played the trumpet, which he called a *horn*. During our lunch breaks, he told me about going into New York City at night to play clubs, putting his name on a list and hoping he got called to the stage. Hoping he knew the tune they called out.

He never called them *songs*. They were *tunes*.

You get up there and the band leader calls a tune, and you just have to know it, he said. You have to be sharp.

Andrew worried he was losing his sharpness. Fewer clubs. Fewer bands. His neighbors complained whenever he played, so he started going to Golden Gate Park at night to practice scales and solos in the artificial forest, where his sounds were drowned out by the waterfall.

. . . .

Andrew told me he was once paid to play jazz on a street corner in his college town in Ohio because the town had wanted to seem more *cultured*. He was supposed to appear to be playing for the loose change of passersby but received an hourly wage.

. . . .

Once, Andrew and I were having beers at a café on Balboa Street and while standing in line for another beer he began flirting with the woman in line behind him. She asked what he did, and Andrew said he was a musician. I could hear them from the table and thought to myself, *Bullshit you are. You work in an office, same as me.*

But I admired what he heard in the question.

She had said, What do you do?

He heard, What do you love to do?

. . . .

Andrew tried to teach me about jazz.

Why Hank Mobley and Freddie Hubbard were geniuses.

Why it was such a tragedy that Clifford Brown died so young.

That Clifford Brown was doing it right.

That Clifford Brown avoided the substances that kept killing jazz musicians.

He lived clean.

He focused on the art.

He died in a car accident on the Pennsylvania Turnpike at age twenty-five.

I said I had never heard of him. *Exactly,* Andrew said. *You would've though.*

Andrew explained that not all jazz is improvised.

That not much jazz is improvised.

That perpetual spontaneity is not the point.

You have to know the standards.

You have to know what to play when you're called to the stage.

You have to begin the tune from somewhere, together.

You have to begin with a kind of mutual precision, a mutual belief in the beauty of the tune, which eventually means taking the tune beyond itself, and this beyondness requires live creativity.

More is possible, but it must be brought into the room anew.

It must be brought into the room every single time.

It must be what you love to do.

Central Crossings

One day Andrew announced he had gotten a new job as an office manager for a start-up.

One day Tyler announced he had gotten a new job as an office manager for a start-up.

One day a Boeing 777 crashed into the tarmac at San Francisco International, which is built on the edge of the peninsula. Runway 28L stretches out over the bay, and the plane's landing gear and tail clipped the seawall. The tail and both engines broke off, and the plane skidded down the runway. Jessica and I watched the pillar of smoke from our living room. The broken aircraft remained in place while the crash was investigated. Flights continued to land on Runway 28L, taxiing past the wreckage in which 3 people had been killed and 187 injured. One person had been ejected from the plane and run over by a fire truck responding to the flames. The driver of the truck hadn't seen the person because so much foam had been sprayed at the crash by other trucks, and the person died concealed in the foam.

One day Jessica and I moved to a college town in Oregon where I was paid to teach writing at a land-grant university. One student, older than me by two decades, wrote about how his spouse had died in a motorcycle crash. One student wrote about growing up near the Bakken oil fields amid a culture of unrelenting sexual violence. One student wrote about the joy of surfing. I never knew if I was helping. I never knew if I was doing what I was being paid to do. Sometimes their writing improved, but sometimes it didn't. The older student, who wrote about his spouse dying, was often frustrated with me, because I never told him if I *liked* his writing. I told him what I thought he was trying to achieve and how he might continue going about it.

But that's not what he wanted to know.

He wanted to know if I liked it.

We disagreed about what I was being paid to do.

After teaching, I was paid to do administrative work at a homeless shelter. The shelter was on a side street of a side street, behind a corn dog factory which was behind a faux-Mexican fast food restaurant. People who had lived in the town for decades had no idea what street I was talking about. They had no idea what building I meant. You had to drive over a little bridge to get there. It was next to the train tracks. By the Toyota dealership. The tributary of a powerful river crossed through the shelter's backyard, which flooded every time it rained.

Threat: *flooding.*

Weakness: *homeless population nearby.*

Threat: *new low-income housing.*

Jessica worked there too, writing grants. She worked down the hall. The shelter was upstairs from us and we could hear when the kids woke up and started moving around, their feet pounding between us.

The university's volleyball team brought holiday presents for the kids.

The football team brought free tickets to their games.

Fraternity men came for a tour—they were planning a fundraiser for the shelter and first wanted to learn about its programs. When the men heard we were looking for donations of winter coats, they began to remove the coats they were wearing. They took off their jackets. They pulled their sweatshirts over their heads and said, Here. You can have these. They made a pile of coats. One of them asked, Do you need shoes? And started to take off his shoes.

I was paid to share this story on social media. I almost cried while I wrote it.

Maybe that's silly.

Maybe it was nothing.

Compare their generosity with their privilege.

Compare the coats they gave with the castle they lived in.

And yet. I still love what they did.

And I hope the men are still like that.

I hope they are like that more often than once.

I hope they are constantly prepared to offer whatever they have right now, right now.

. . . .

Part of my job was human resources, and one day a shelter assistant was fired. I don't remember why, but I remember disagreeing with the decision. Courtney worked the overnight shift, the same job Jessica had worked eight years before in Iowa City. Courtney's manager waited to fire her at the end of a shift, at 8 A.M., a tactic I also disagreed with. Courtney was exhausted, and then she was unemployed. She came to my office and sat in a wheely chair and cried for thirty minutes. She told me this was her first job out of college. How was she going to pay rent? How was she going to buy food? How was she going to get a new job in social services if she was fired from her very first job in social services? The office cat circled the wheels of her chair. She was going to miss the cat. I nodded. I listened. I ordered her last paycheck from the finance office and then left the job for a different one.

One day at my new job, I was taking money to the bank, and Courtney was my teller.

She looked miserable.

Probably not because she worked at a bank.

Probably because I had just walked into it.

. . . .

One day at my new job, I received a text message from Jessica that the shelter was on lockdown. My new office was between the shelter and the police department, and police vehicles started zooming past.

City police.

Sheriff deputies.

State police.

A man had brought a gun into the corn dog factory and started firing.

I logged onto a Facebook group where people who owned police scanners reported all the stuff that was happening on the scanner. A SWAT team was brought in. The Toyota dealership was being locked down. The faux-Mexican restaurant was evacuated.

Then it was done. The SWAT team members did what they were paid to do. The man was arrested. No one was injured. The next day, the newspaper reported how certain nearby businesses were evacuated or locked down. The newspaper did not mention the shelter, even though it was the nearest building to the factory and the only nearby building where people lived. Even though the shelter was in the factory's backyard. Between the factory and the creek.

It was in that backyard so we wouldn't have to think about it.

When people decide to forget about something, they are often successful.

. . . .

One day at my new job, I was paid to attend a training designed to help nonprofits prepare for the Cascadia Subduction Zone earthquake, also known as the Really Big One. The idea was that nonprofits would be important in responding to the catastrophe because they are already adept at serving people in crisis, people who need emergency food or shelter or clothing.

The training was in Eugene, and a man in the audience suggested that Eugene should prepare for an influx of people fleeing the tsunami-devastated coastline. The trainer shook his head. The trainer said, No. You don't need to prepare for an influx. Nobody will be *fleeing* the coast. People on the coast who survive will not be able to flee because the mountains of the Coast Range will be impassable.

The bridges will have all collapsed.

The roads will have ruptured.

Every community will be an island.

What we are talking about right now is rescuing each other.

Your literal neighbor.

That is the most you will be able to do.

It is still a lot to have to do.

Some in the audience volunteered that they had trained in first aid.

Some had learned to triage a mass-casualty event.

Some had experience communicating with satellite phones, because of the recent blizzards.

Some had experience evacuating the elderly, whose homes had been threatened by the recent fires.

We talked about transportation issues that had arisen during the recent flood.

I'm just saying you have to stay sharp.

You have to stay sharp for a lot of reasons.

You have to know what to play when your name is picked from the list.

When the bandleader calls a tune.

The tune is only the beginning.

Whatever you prepared for is only the beginning.

Whatever you prepared for you have to exceed.

You have to corkscrew your torso to the piano as an intentional display of strength.

You have to arrive at the present with some enthusiasm.

You have to have a good attitude to live in a world like this.

You have to love it.

True North

Indigenous communities of Ioway, Omaha, Sac, Meskwaki, Sioux, and Otoe knew the place first, for hundreds of years, before the French claimed it as theirs, then the Spanish, and then again the French, who ceded it to the United States so that white Americans first knew it as part of the territory of Louisiana, then knew it as the territory of Missouri, then the territory of Michigan, then the territory of Wisconsin, then the territory of Iowa, until finally its admission to the union as the state of Iowa in 1846, just thirty-eight years before Nettie Ray was born.

Nettie Ray was born in Illinois in 1884 and moved to Iowa at age three. She was my wife's great-grandmother, and she began recording her journal a hundred years ago. The entries begin in South Dakota in 1920, where she and her husband Albert had moved, and continue through 1931 after they returned to western Iowa to farm, and onward through 1954. Many of the entries are about weather—wind, blizzards, subzero cold—or the farm: the selling price of calves, pigs, hens, corn, cream, potatoes, eggs. The cost of plums, watermelon, flour. The cost of fixing a dress. In the journal, Nettie records her hopes, her observations, her joys, her concerns about war and winter and drought and sickness. Sometimes she writes half a page and sometimes a couple of words.

May 29, 1921: "It rained."

May 30, 1921: "At home."

June 6, 1921: "Rained last night."

June 15, 1921: "Has been raining most of the time since Sunday night. The creek down at Fellows came up in a hurry, washed away their hog house and grainery, Water was in the house 3 ft. deep. Albert went down and helped them—what he could."

It's kind of a joke how often midwesterners discuss the weather, but tell that to Nettie. Tell her the zone between earth and outer space—the layers of clash between heaven and the terrestrial, an arrangement so fragile and rare it allows for life nowhere else in the solar system, an arrangement so unpredictably violent it can eradicate a year of crops, or a day of work, or a grainery—is unworthy of her attention. I hear in her commentary about the weather a reverence for place. Her fingers on its pulse. Every word about the cold implies a humbleness. Implies the unsympathetic force of her environment. It is always up there, and she knows to look up and see it.

. . . .

My eighth grade Iowa history teacher, Mr. Olson, liked to take us on field trips to the cemetery. Mr. Olson was tall and bald with a long gray scraggly beard, and he sometimes stored pencils inside his beard to amuse us. The cemetery was across the street from the junior high. He taught us where to walk. He taught us the word *mausoleum*. He said it was important that we referred to the tombstones as *grave markers*. He prohibited our use of *like* as a filler word. If you were speaking in class and said *like* . . . , he would interrupt you with a gesture and you had to start over. He taught us that Iowa used to be swampland. He taught us about magnetic fields. He carried a walking stick and moved around the cemetery at a hustle. We chased after him and complained about it. He treated the cemetery like a classroom. He treated history like environmental science: every place was a laboratory.

Sometimes Mr. Olson would bring old, unusual objects to class and make us ask yes/no questions about the object until we understood its purpose. One day he brought in something that looked like a hairbrush.

Aaron asked, Is it a hairbrush?

No.

Is it a hairbrush for an animal?

No.

We kept guessing, badly, so Mr. Olson recommended widening the scope of our inquiry. Maybe ask if the object is used in a certain kind of building or in a certain room. Start wide and then narrow it down.

Is it used in the bathroom?

No.

Is it used in the bedroom?

No.

Is it used in the kitchen?

Yes.

That was as close as we got. No further questions were productive, and eventually Mr. Olson grew agitated and just told us: The object punches holes into crackers. It's a *docker*. Back when crackers were made by hand, the docker punctured the dough to release trapped air so the air wouldn't expand and explode while the dough baked.

I'd never considered that people made crackers before factories did.

I'd forgotten crackers had holes.

I'd noticed but not really noticed.

The final exam for Iowa history required us to memorize all the major towns in the state, all the major rivers and lakes, and all ninety-nine counties and then stand in front of a large map at the front of the class and find as many as we could in two minutes. The names were printed on little slips and commingled in a fishbowl, and we drew them out one by one, pointed to the map, and said, *Maquoketa! Skunk River! Winneshiek County! Clinton County! Indianola!* The fishbowl test was about history insofar as it was about orientation. The rest of the class turned their desks to give the test taker a sense of privacy, but you could hear how fast the person went. You could hear them pause. Silence meant they were lost.

. . . .

Nettie was conflicted about her family's return to Iowa from South Dakota. In October 1932, she writes,

> Albert has the blues and I sure feel blue too, we had another letter
> from the insurance loan company today. They want us to pay it. But
> it's sure hard to make up our money when everything is so cheap
> and last spring our pigs all died. I guess we only saved 14. I don't
> know what things are coming to but I do hope we don't have to lose
> our home it makes me feel heart sick and think if we had only had
> staid in Dakota. But I guess a person never knows what is best. But
> I guess we should have left well enough alone and been satisfied to
> stay there.

She regrets leaving.

She then forgives herself for leaving, because a person never knows what is best.

She then seems immediately confident about what is best.

We should have left well enough alone.

One year later, in October 1933, Nettie writes, "Started for Dakota to go to Uncle Henry's funeral. Started home Friday noon. Dakota is surely a barren looking place. No crops at all. Didn't even raise their chicken feed on account of drought and grasshoppers. Sure glad we are not living there."

. . . .

Once, Mr. Olson took us on a daylong field trip of the county, promising that whoever could retrace our exact route would receive an A for the whole class, so we began the bus ride with maps and stared diligently through the windows, but the early morning was dark and we soon lost track of the turns.

. . . .

Recently, my spouse and I were sitting in a family member's living room, talking about politics, which at the time meant discussing statues of Confederate generals, some of which were being removed from public spaces in the South.

Jessica and I were in Iowa, where we both grew up, back from the college town in western Oregon where we live now. The juxtaposition between these places had begun to feel more and more distressing—the distance between our mostly liberal northwest town and the mostly conservative midwestern place we came from. Political pundits lamented what we felt as *polarization* and *divisiveness* in America, though I had been thinking about it more as *homesickness*: when you feel home pulling away from you while you're still a part of it.

Sitting on a red faux-leather couch, I said that taking down the statues was the right thing to do. My relative, reclined in a sofa chair, scoffed. You know who *also* likes to tear down statues? he said. You know who *also* likes to destroy culture? The Taliban. They destroy culture. They destroy history. Ripping down statues is exactly what the Taliban would do. He continued: And who's next? Thomas Jefferson owned slaves. Is he next? Are you going to remove him from history? How about George Washington? Are you going to erase George Washington?

. . . .

Nettie reports that in February 1934, she and Albert attended a spelling contest. Albert failed on the word *cruiser*. At the time, the word usually referred to a naval vessel. Usage of it had become more common during World War I and would soon revive again. Nettie failed on the word *quandary*, which was also undergoing a bump in popular usage, though it's harder to pin down why.

. . . .

I grew up in a town named for George Washington within a county also named for him, though the county was once named for someone else. Washington County was first called Slaughter County, after William Slaughter, the secretary of the Wisconsin Territory from 1837 to 1841, when the territory included present-day Iowa, much of Minnesota, and part of the Dakotas. The name Slaughter County lasted barely a year; local residents "abhorred" the name, according to one history, and petitioned for something different.

In his autobiography, William Slaughter speculates about where his name might have originated. He wasn't sure of the source exactly, but he knew English names sometimes came from occupations: people named Smith were blacksmiths or gunsmiths or goldsmiths or locksmiths. People named Shoemaker. People named Baker. So William considered that his own surname might've originated that way, though he didn't know who or what his ancestors might've slaughtered: "If they slew whole regiments of men, they were warriors or heroes; if only a few individuals, they were murderers; if they slew innocent brutes they were butchers. We infer from the motto on the family coat of arms . . . that they were warriors. . . . If their propensities were ever warlike, they have been thoroughly eradicated by the arts of peace and the meliorating influences of civilization."

William Slaughter inferred that he came from a lineage of soldiers, a lineage that had evolved from a favoring of violence to a favoring of peace. Slaughter himself was an attorney. But his name implied something different, so for the county, the attorney's name that connoted violence was rejected in favor of the president and military general's name that connoted cleanliness. Slaughter turned to Washington. It strikes me as an attempt at sanitization. The word *Washington* has a certain decorum. It carries the undertones of both war and enslavement, absolutisms of violence and power, inside a word that feels stately. Distinguished. *Washington*. The etymology suggests a man from the estate of Wassa, a place in England, which means the place I am from is named for a man who is most famous for leading a violent separation from the place he is named for. Probably some of the atmospheric stateliness of *Washington* comes from its connotation with England, the implied upper-class whiteness. The implied hedgerows. The implied silverware.

Something maybe obvious but strange about being a transplant is the way you have to start over learning the history. The part of your identity that forms in response to geography duplicates, which means the part of your identity that forms in response to history duplicates. I'm never done with Iowa, but I'm not living within it as directly anymore, and now the past of another place floats around me, and these manifold pasts begin to form layers—troposphere, stratosphere, and so on—and the layers of past are different for each person and they are creating your conditions even when you don't understand how.

The town where I live now also has a history of changing its name. Corvallis was founded as Marysville in 1849, likely continuing the tradition of French fur trappers who had named a nearby mountain after the Virgin Mary. Marysville became Corvallis in 1853. In the middle of Oregon's long Willamette Valley, *Corvallis* means the "heart of the valley." The man who founded Corvallis and supposedly coined its name, Joseph Avery, recently had his own name removed from a building on the campus of the local university. Joseph Avery owned a printing press, which produced a proslavery newspaper. Avery may have had an editorial role in its message. He advertised on its pages. The paper repeatedly argued that Oregon should legalize the enslavement of Black people. A local park and nature center are still named for Joseph Avery, and the town is named for him, in a way. It was his idea that the valley was a body and we were its heart.

During the mid-nineteenth century, when Avery's paper argued for the enslavement of Black people, Oregon was a "free" state, though Oregon's version of freedom was mostly meaningless. Enslavement was illegal, but it was also illegal for Black people to live in Oregon, so that historically Oregon failed to even conceive of free Black people: either they existed to be enslaved, or they were not allowed to exist here at all. The Oregon Constitution stated, "No free negro, or mulatto, not residing in this state at the time of the adoption of this constitution, shall come, reside, or be within this State, or hold any real estate." The passage became legally obsolete after the Civil War but remained in the constitution until 1926, when 62 percent of voters agreed to remove it.

The poet and historian Walidah Imarisha puts it this way: "Oregon's very foundation was as a white homeland, a white nation-state. This is a place where white folks could come and get away from the issues of the day, which were seen to be tied to the presence of people of color. Come here and get away from that and build the white homeland, the white utopia that you dream of." This reminds me of the author Jennine Capó Crucet, who writes in her book of essays *My Time among the Whites*, "When I speak at other predominantly white campuses, I've reminded the students of color and the women about this fact: This place never imagined you here, and your exclusion was a fundamental premise of its initial design."

This place could refer to all of Oregon.

The writer Mitchell Jackson has argued that one ongoing dilemma with the white-supremacist history of Oregon is the degree to which its founders succeeded in their vision. The degree to which their success has *held*. Imagine those early white legislators looking around now at, say, Corvallis, where Black people make up 1.1 percent of the population. Imagine the satisfaction they might feel. "This is actually of a plan," Jackson tells David Naimon, of Portland's Tin House. "And all these years later, a hundred and seventy years later, it's working."

. . . .

In advance of the 2000 presidential election, Mr. Olson conducted an informal poll of our class, asking our favorite candidate. He made us do the thing where we put our heads down on our desks and wrapped one arm around to make a little pocket so we couldn't see, and then we raised the other hand. After we voted, he told us how the results often predicted the way our county would vote because our parents had passed down their politics to us. I don't remember how I voted, but I remember every nonconformist teenager in the room was offended—just aghast—at the notion that our beliefs had come to us from our *parents*.

. . . .

"We're told history is linear," says Walidah Imarisha in a lecture about Oregon's white supremacist history. "I think history is a spiral. It's not a circle. We're not in the exact same place, but we can look up and see it if we know to look up. We've had these conversations before."

In a video of the lecture, Imarisha traces the shape of history's spiral in the air as she describes it.

The trajectory of the spiral is downward.

We can look up and see it if we know to look up.

I like the idea that the past is above us like a contrail in the sky.

The past above us like weather.

I like the idea of history as a downward spiral.

It's not nihilism so much as humility.

. . . .

One time in class, Mr. Olson became aware that many of us teenagers were unskilled with cardinal directions, so we had to place our heads down on our desks again.

Okay, said Mr. Olson, everyone point *north*.

After we stopped pointing and raised our heads, he looked at us in amazement.

We have a lot of work to do, he said. Most of you were wrong, and some of you pointed *up*.

. . . .

Once, a reporter from CBS, for a segment called "Everybody Has a Story," threw a dart at a map of the United States and hit Washington, Iowa. The reporter traveled to Washington, stopped at the first payphone, opened to a random page, picked a random number, called it, asked to interview the man who answered, drove to the man's house, and talked to him about his life. In the segment, the guy from the phone book—his name is Guy—enjoys a life of fishing. "I just love to fish," says Guy. "I fish in the spring, I fish in the fall, I fish in the winter. I like to fish all the time if I can." The premise of *everybody has a story* requires that Guy be more remarkable than his love for fishing, so the reporter pressed him, and eventually Guy revealed he was nearly killed in a mortar attack at age twenty-two in Vietnam.

Guy and a buddy had dug a foxhole, but two sergeants came along and took it from them.

Mortars hit the position soon after, and both sergeants were killed.

In the segment, the one fact about Guy is a response to the other. Guy loves the tranquility of fishing *because* he so narrowly survived a war.

Violence drew him closer to peace.

Its meliorating influence.

The segment aired on August 22, 2001.

. . . .

Nettie Ray describes going to church on the morning of December 7, 1941. "It wasn't a very nice day—windy and dusty." There was a bridal shower in the morning. Thirty-five people came. Gifts nicer than she had ever seen. "But something awful happened today."

Days later, she reports that Germany, Italy, and the United States have declared war on each other. She closes the year by writing, "It snowed all day and I think it's still snowing but maybe it won't amount to much."

There are no entries in 1942 or 1943.

. . . .

It wasn't a very nice day—windy and dusty. The word *dusty* now reminds me of how Dusty used to be the name of a small town just south of where I live. I don't know for certain why in the early twentieth century its name changed to Bellfountain; the local histories only speculate on the change. My own speculation is that someone looked at a sign that said DUSTY and thought, For Chrissake, how about we do better than that?

. . . .

The payphone the reporter used for "Everybody Has a Story" belonged to the gas station my family owns, on the edge of Washington. My aunt was working when the van pulled up, and she watched the cameraman film the phone from a lot of different angles—she couldn't believe how much footage they needed just of the phone—and finally during a break she asked if that big camera was *heavy*, it looks so heavy, and the man said, Here, feel my shoulder, and my aunt ran her hand along the ledge of his body and marveled at how the camera had produced a hard, thick knob beside his neck, a great callous. How he'd changed to bear the weight.

. . . .

Corvallis is a college town, and college towns are sites of perpetual tension. They are little hubs of polarization. They are radiant with homesickness.

In 1878, William Slaughter published an essay about his favorite college town, Madison, Wisconsin. Madison is like Corvallis in that it's home to a land-grant university—an educational center founded to serve rural concerns. Slaughter described the city of Madison as an improvement on Rome: more intellectual, more beautiful, better governed, better planned. He praised the libraries, hotels, and churches, the capitol building, the skilled professionals, the excellent food. He liked the proximity to nature. He liked how nature was so full of birds. He loved the birds' music—the "thrilling" partridge, the "plaintive" dove, the "warlike scream" of eagles. Slaughter praised the college town for its commitment to progress. He compared the university students favorably to Rome's gladiators, fighting in the arena of discourse, triumphing at commencement. Slaughter believed

Madison had struck the ultimate balance of power and peace. It had strong defenses and strong schools. It had partridges and eagles. He explained the city's population of 12,000 was "enough to secure the advantage of the cities, and not enough to incur their evils."

He is stating a balance between the rewards and limits of community—between the point when community really gets going and the point when it becomes unmanageable. His affection for place is cautionary, a goodness that must be carefully protected. It's the way some people in Corvallis talk about our own college town, which is constantly in danger of becoming too much like Portland. Many people here, white people especially, like this town the way it is. They like the nearby forest and the farmers' market. They like the annual art show on the courthouse lawn, where retirees sell watercolors of Oregon landscapes. They like downtown, where the no-chain ordinance promotes small businesses, where restaurants serve burgers with local beef and Tillamook cheese. There are three independent bookstores. Three different bike shops. For a while, you could buy secondhand LEGOs from two different stores within four blocks of each other. This part of town appears *quaint* to a certain white perspective, and a tremendous effort has been made to create and preserve the quaintness.

Maybe Slaughter was going overboard when he compared Madison to Rome, but some folks in Corvallis have an overstated comparison about their own town.

They call it Camelot.

. . . .

Recently, I was running with a group in the forest. We ran the same mountain every Thursday night. Me. An attorney. A hairdresser. An engineer. An instructor from the fisheries department. A social worker. A college student. And so forth. We were an hour deep into the forest, and Maria was saying it would be nice if a certain trail race could raise money for scholarships—school was so expensive—and she especially wanted to help students who couldn't apply for other funding. For certain reasons. Certain students who couldn't apply. She wasn't quite saying what she meant, and the attorney said, It's okay. You're among friends. And she finally allowed, You know, kids from undocumented families. And something kind of clicked into place—how Corvallis is maybe a *nice liberal college town*, but still not the kind of place where you can know right away if you are among friends.

One week, we had stopped at a midpoint up the mountain. A spot where people could turn around if they were on a tight schedule. If they have to feed the dog or start dinner. People were heading back, so that Kim, another man, another woman, and I were the only ones left. Then the woman changed her mind, so it was just one other man, Kim, and I. Noticing this, Kim changed her mind. She no longer wanted to go farther into the forest. She scrambled to think of a reason. And I started to understand the reason was that she couldn't be sure if she was among friends. And I started to understand how the self-image of a place is often a form of gaslighting. The quaintness. The Northwest Nice. Corvallis has a lot of pride about being one of the safest towns in America. As Eula Biss has said, "We could begin by understanding ourselves as dangerous."

. . . .

I pointed up. It was me. I should just say it. When Mr. Olson asked the class to point north, I was one of the kids who pointed up. Maybe the only kid. Maybe he said *some of you pointed up*, implying a group, to ease the blow. I wanted this essay to include Mr. Olson's reaction to this mistake without the mistake being mine, but I remember that moment in a strange way, more than the embarrassment. More than the accident of thinking. I remember the moment when a thing I knew became a thing I *really* knew.

When a thing I knew became a thing I felt.

The moment when I understood the map looked different from within it. The map looked different from down in here, and I looked out the classroom window toward the cemetery and thought *west* and there was almost a spin to it.

A warp.

It felt kind of like vertigo.

And at the same time it felt like an *alignment*.

. . . .

Recently, Oregon State Police released body cam footage showing the arrest of a student on the Oregon State campus. The arrest has been controversial. The trooper stopped a young woman for allegedly riding her bicycle on the wrong side of a quiet residential street near campus. When the trooper asked for her identification, she refused to provide it. The situation escalated. Footage of the encounter lasts thirty-eight minutes and shows the woman standing in the grassy right-of-way while young people gather at a distance to watch. A cruiser is parked in the background. The tone of the conversation is tense but measured. The distrust between the woman and the man is seismic. She repeatedly declines to provide her identification and tries to explain her skepticism of his authority. He interrupts her, and she says, "Please let me finish what I have to say, sir."

"Go ahead," he says.

"You have to understand, people who look like me are often—"

He interrupts again: "What do you look like? You keep saying that. I don't understand what you look like. How do you look any different from me?"

She explains to him that she is a woman.

She explains her skin is darker than his.

She explains her body is more petite, her frame is smaller.

And for these reasons, the way people respond to her as she moves through the world is different from the way people respond to him.

By then, another officer has arrived, from the Corvallis Police Department. The trooper tells the student he is going to arrest her and reaches to grab her arms. She recoils and the two men tackle her. One straddles her body, which is supine, and wrenches her arm until the wrenching forces her into the prone position. Both men kneel atop her. One handcuffs her, pressing his knees into her back and legs, pinning her to the grass. After the men stand, she stays lying face down, handcuffed, and eventually asks to sit. The officers approach to haul her up, but the woman doesn't want to be touched and struggles away, so they wrestle her back onto the grass.

After the incident, a wave of op-eds appeared in the local newspaper, critical of the student for her behavior during the arrest, critical of the university for defending her, and critical of the NAACP for releasing a statement that condemned law enforcement's handling of the situation.

One community member said the woman failed to show a "modicum of respect."

Another called the student a "rude, entitled brat of a young woman."

Another said she "needs some manners, a binky and a time out in her room for a week."

Another said she "created a situation she could weaponize" like "Jussie Smollett in Chicago."

Another sought to assure readers that "this is not a race issue."

Another said it was "not a racial bias incident."

Another said the NAACP was "playing the race card."

Several complained the woman had insulted the officer with her non-compliance: "Do not insult the uniform or their authority unless you want Corvallis to become Portland, Los Angeles, Seattle, or New York City."

Of course, I'm not worried Corvallis will become Portland. I'm worried Corvallis has too effectively become itself.

. . . .

Mr. Olson once told us that a certain apartment building near the junior high school had a flat roof because the man who built it was then in the process of inventing the helicopter. Long before the Wright brothers, the man was a visionary and decided to exhibit his machine to the townspeople to teach them about the possibilities of flight. He brought his machine to the fairgrounds, but the people were skeptical—the idea of a helicopter is ridiculous if you have never heard of a helicopter—and they feared that this man would ruin the public image of the community, make them all seem foolish, so they sabotaged his vehicle. They destroyed it. And he didn't have the resources to start over, so Washington did not become First in Flight, though it still has one building with a flat roof upon which the inventor never had a chance to land.

The story begs to be interpreted as a parable for the town's conservatism—the new is dangerous and the dangerous is torn apart—but it also emphasizes within that dynamic the role of reputation. The machine was no threat or burden to the community, but it was not how they viewed themselves. They hated the machine because it failed to produce their own reflection.

. . . .

Nettie on June 8, 1944: "It has rained most all day and it's cloudy yet tonight and cold. We have fire in furnace. Amelia Fletcher came and got Phyllis she wants P. to fix her hair. Cora called up after dinner said to come up as Ella was up there. So Phyllis, Mildred and I went up. Have just been listening to the news. Fierce fighting where invasion taking place."

Mildred was my wife's grandmother and we used to visit her at the nursing home in Des Moines. She hated leaving the farm in western Iowa. She resented her little room in Des Moines, but she sat with us and visited. She was a reader and always demanded that my wife and I read *The Kite Runner* and its sequel. She always demanded to know our thoughts on the pipeline. She was always concerned about the construction of pipelines. The taking of land distressed her. In 2017, my wife and I flew back to Iowa for her funeral, and during the service someone told a story about Mildred being sick near the very end. The doctor wanted to gauge her lucidity and asked, Who is the president right now? Mildred nearly spat at him the answer. When I think about Nettie, when I try to understand the ways that place floated up through her life, I remember Mildred and I remember how her thinking was not governed by stereotypes—that she, as a white woman on rural farmland in the Midwest, had her own personality. She had her own views on things.

That same trip back to Iowa, I was in a living room for a family thing and my uncle asked my dad about the pipeline. What would you do? he asked. If it was your land? The hypothetical bothered me, because it erased the most important fact of the situation; the whole point was that the land did not belong to a white person. For once. Yet. The whole point was that it did not belong to someone like my dad. It belonged to people with a different perspective on history. People who looked up into the sky of the past and saw it differently. But Dad smiled and said, I'd cash the check.

· ·

The county where I'm from in Iowa includes a township called Oregon. I lived in the Oregon Township of Washington County, Iowa, for the first few years of my life, though I didn't know it at the time. I didn't know what townships were until Mr. Olson taught us about them in eighth grade. Recently I learned that the Oregon Township had once been called Long Creek, but in 1847 a man named J. L. L. Terry decided to change its name. Terry had always wanted to keep moving. He had wanted to reach Oregon but never did, so he rechristened the place where he lived to match the place he wanted to live. The history I'm reading doesn't say *why* Terry wanted to reach Oregon, or what Oregon meant to him in 1847, what idea it contained that he decided to impose back onto Iowa.

If he envied the new white homeland.

If to him Oregon meant *frontier* or *freedom*, and if it meant *freedom*, what that meant.

· ·

In many places around Oregon, *Portland* is a pejorative. In the rural space around Corvallis, *Corvallis* is a pejorative. *Eugene* is a pejorative in most places outside of Eugene. Often the names of these places signify *out of touch*. Or by the way the names are spoken you hear *progressive*, which is also a pejorative. In many ways, Oregon is an especially polarized state. University of Oregon political science professor Priscilla Southwell recently described the state as a "perfect storm" of divisiveness: the metro areas of

Portland, Salem, Corvallis, and Eugene all share the Willamette Valley, while on the eastern side of the Cascade Mountains, in the vast high desert, lie places like Wheeler County, which is the size of Delaware but so sparsely populated that it has no hospital, doctors, dentists, optometrists, or professional paramedics. Technically, Wheeler County is more rural than rural: the Oregon Office of Rural Health defines places with fewer than 6 people per square mile as *frontier*.

Portland is home to 4,500 people per square mile.

Corvallis is home to 133 people per square mile.

Wheeler County's population per square mile is less than 1.

Frontier is superlative rural.

Frontier implies a different kind of life.

It's hard to say what people in Wheeler County have in common with people in Portland or Corvallis. Sometimes it's hard to say what people in Corvallis have in common with people in Corvallis.

Some folks decided to find out.

. . . .

The Oregon Values and Beliefs Project began in 1992 with the goal of better understanding what held the state together, what joined the metro and the rural, the conservative and the liberal, the varying demographics of this vast western geography. The project takes the form of an elaborate survey, conducted every ten years, most recently in 2013. It is guided by these questions: "What do we most value in our social and political lives? What do we think is working well, and what are our concerns? How do we view pressing issues such as governance and taxes, health care, education, jobs and the environment?" The 2013 study included more than 9,000 Oregonians from across the state. The results were compiled in a document called *True North*, presumably because the results intended to illuminate who we are and the direction we are going together. It seems worth noting that *True North* is a response to polarization but it also *means* polarization. The furthest thing from the idea of compromise, true north is one of the poles, which means our vocabularies for unity and division draw on the same metaphor *in the same way*.

The project asserts that about three-quarters of Oregonians believe in health and personal responsibility—that one should take care of one's body rather than rely on a medical industry to repair its damage. A slight majority favors protecting the environment, even if that protection slows the local economy. Two-thirds agree that incarcerated people should be rehabilitated during their incarceration. More than 80 percent agree with the statement "Oregonians from diverse backgrounds should work together to solve problems." Some of these things don't really feel like a victory. The *True North* document asserts that 86 percent of Oregonians believe *taxes are necessary to pay for the common good*, which means people were polled about the most basic feature of the society they live in, and in eastern Oregon 17 percent disagreed with the idea of taxes at all. The rate of agreement drops when the tax gets specific: more than a quarter of Oregonians don't want to share the cost of fixing roads; barely half agree on the idea of sharing the cost of public transportation; less than half agree on the idea of paying for new roads and highways. I had thought infrastructure was the cliché topic for bipartisan agreement. That no matter what we disagreed about, we could still agree to maintain the bridges.

· ·

My coworker tells me the student could've made the whole thing stop.

She could've cooperated.

She could've handed over her ID.

I tell her the officer seemed unprepared for the possibility that some members of his community might distrust him. He seemed unaware that people might be hauling around some distrust. I say carrying a gun in public is a destabilizing thing. It creates an imbalance of power, it creates a lot of fear, and the person carrying the gun is responsible for correcting that imbalance, they have to fix the problem, because they brought the gun to the situation and created all the fear.

She can see I'm getting kind of heated about it.

She says, Well, that makes me think the officers need more training. About how to resolve a situation.

My coworker's politics are very different from mine, and I think this is as close to an agreement as we're going to get.

· ·

June 12, 1944: "It rained awful again today, fairly flooded my garden. So much dirt from that south field washed into the garden and yard and water and mud ran into the basement again."

It rained the day of Mildred's funeral, which took place in western Iowa, not far from the land Nettie writes about. The limousine that was supposed to transport family from the church to the cemetery wouldn't start, so someone pulled a truck alongside and the pastor in his suit hustled through the rain. He popped both hoods and leaned over the limousine engine with the cables. I can't remember why Mr. Olson wanted us to call them *grave markers* instead of *tombstones*. If his concern was about connotation. If *tombstone* signaled the film, the fetishized historical violence. If *marker* pointed more to the person. Mildred's plot in the cemetery is on a hill overlooking the sloping fields. The place is beautiful even in the grayness of the rain, and I remember looking out from the hill to the surrounding fields and wondering if part of what felt so beautiful about the land was knowing how much she had loved it.

The *True North* document states that 78 percent of Oregonians, when asked an open-ended question about what they value in the state, referred to the natural environment. They referred to the mountains, forests, clean air, waterways. Sometimes the land meant beauty, and sometimes it meant independence or liberty. Sometimes it meant timber, livestock, lavender, pinot noir. Sometimes mountain biking, skiing, canoeing, hiking. Maybe this is not surprising. The survey asked people, What do you value about living here? And the people began describing the place around them. They began describing *here*.

One day Mr. Olson taught us how to turn apples into cider. We pressed the apples at a long table in the school parking lot and then brought the cider inside to drink at our desks. Each of us sat with our one cup. Aaron noted how dirty it looked. Hailey also wondered if it was safe to drink. It didn't look clean. Is it clean? Mr. Olson looked back at us. You tell me, he said. *You* made it.

And we all thought back to what we had just done.

Something that gives me pause but also gives me energy is how the polarities of a country arise from individuals who contain some of those polarities within themselves. The United States is polarized between its coasts and its middle, and many of us who have lived in both places are influenced by both experiences. Which is only to say polarization is both an exterior and an interior event. That some of the conflicts and tensions we witness we also embody. Each point on the map, each node on the chart, is miles deep. Years deep. Each point on the map is itself a map. Each node on the chart itself a chart. This gives me both energy and pause.

Recently, a man who was in town from Eugene told me he appreciated Corvallis's downtown area. Its cleanliness. He said in Eugene you're basically stepping over hippies and homeless people. But here it's nice. The man was not old enough to remember the 1950s, but regardless he said, It's so nice here it looks straight out of the fifties.

In 1953, Nettie watched the inauguration of President Eisenhower on television. She describes the event as *interesting* but doesn't say why. She is pleased when the next month Eisenhower is baptized for the first time: "He had never belonged to a church before. We were glad to hear that he realizes he needs God in his life. The country is in awful condition. I hope and pray that things will get better and that this awful war will come to an end. Had a letter from Gerald Friday. Said he had taken his physical so I'm afraid he will soon be in army too. Makes us feel so bad, will be so hard for him to be separated from his Phyllis too. Dana is still in Japan."

The country is in awful condition. At most, the student was stubborn. In the video, she asks the trooper to define every word he uses. He uses the term *passive resistance* and she asks him to define what that means. She challenges him on the definition of *vehicle*. Does *vehicle* include *bicycle* and, if it does, how can she trust he is right? She wants to know everything he is doing and what law gives him permission to do it and where is the book containing the law and why doesn't he carry the book with him. They debate what counts as the center of the road. They debate whether each of them is being courteous enough and who is required to be more courteous. She repeats *please* and *sir*. The trooper asks her to define things too. When she says *people who look like me*, he says, *What do you look like? I don't understand what you look like.* They are trying to come to terms, in a way. In a literal way. They are trying to describe the situation to each other. They are speaking across a distance. She is polite but uncooperative. He is patient, then less patient, and then he is on top of her, forcing her body into a painful position—an action he was always empowered to take, which was part of her concern.

Recently, I was reading one of the famous essays by Audre Lorde, published in 1979, where she writes, "Difference must be not merely tolerated but seen as a fund of necessary polarities between which creativity can spark like a dialectic." The essay originated as a lecture at a conference on feminism, and Lorde was frustrated that the conference did not have more Black panelists or lesbian panelists or panelists from developing countries.

She was describing the necessity of a more inclusive feminism, one of class diversity, racial diversity, queer diversity. She was implying to her crowd that they—we—would have to work on more than one problem at a time.

We will need *a fund of necessary polarities.*

We will have to treat those polarities as a dialectic.

In the book, the essay follows a thirty-page interview between Lorde and the white poet and essayist Adrienne Rich. The interview, too, is a dialectic. Rich and Lorde are close, they have an ongoing friendship, but they are trying to attend to the distances between them. Rich wants to know the details of Lorde's struggles in order to understand them. She wants to hear exactly what it's like for Lorde. Rich says,

> There's a way in which, trying to translate from your experience to mine, I do need to hear chapter and verse from time to time. I'm afraid of it all slipping away into, "Ah, yes, I understand you." . . . "Yes, of course we understand each other because we love each other." That's bullshit. So if I ask for documentation, it's because I take seriously the spaces between us that difference has created, that racism has created. There are times when I simply cannot assume that I know what you know, unless you show me what you mean.

Lorde resists a bit: "I'm used to associating a request for documentation as a questioning of my perceptions, an attempt to devalue what I'm in the process of discovering." In a way, detail is proof. Story is proof. It is evidence. You are making a case about your experience. They keep calling it *documentation.* Paperwork that serves to confirm, or clarify, or elucidate the fact of a distance, the experience of living across a polarity. Rich wants enough information to verify for herself the size and shape of the space between them. I think Lorde is saying, Listen, I'm telling you the shape. I've perceived it my whole life.

Rich is concerned about the limits, or the liability, of trust. The point where trust leads in the wrong direction, leads away from understanding, away from knowing. She also understands the quandary of asking for the details of a struggle; it starts to look like the treacherous project of requiring the oppressed person to narrate their oppression to the oppressor. If anyone understands this problem, it's Rich.

I know there are limits to how we can apply Lorde's idea to our own time. Not every polarity is the same. But I do appreciate the idea that polarity can be a source of wealth, a *fund* made of our *necessary* differences—a source of wealth provided that we are willing to learn from the differences.

The first time I read Adrienne Rich's poetry I was deployed to Afghanistan. I had brought along her selected poems and I read some of them while sitting in a Humvee turret on guard duty. The Humvee was parked on a berm overlooking the base entrance, which was rarely used, so I sat up high overlooking a road, waiting for my time to be done. I remember reading again and again the lines "this is the oppressor's language / yet I need it to talk to you." I remember feeling the situation of reading the poems was getting more strange the more I understood what the poems were about. I set the book next to the turret's machine gun and took a picture, to try to visualize for myself this juxtaposition. I read again and again *this is the oppressor's language / yet I need it to talk to you.* Sitting in the turret, I felt alarmed because I had thought the language of the poem was beautiful.

The Frontier

. . . .

I learned from the high school English teacher Mr. Thomas that I should not write *get* in a sentence. What does it mean? he asked our class. To *get* something? Ryan said it meant like to *have*. Like to acquire. Mr. Thomas had predicted this response and replied, So if I tell you to please get the door, could you get the door, that means I want you to go *have* the door? Bring me the door? Ryan looked irritated while Mr. Thomas looked satisfied that he made his point, which was not to avoid words with multiple definitions but to choose words on purpose, and *get* was an instinct, not a decision. Mr. Thomas wanted us to understand that we were supposed to think about writing as creating sentences with words in them and each word mattered a lot, and I admit I found this idea pretty intriguing.

Mr. Thomas taught us about the prince and the ghost and asked the question about madness.

He taught us a Hawthorne story about a man who fell asleep beneath a tree and things happened around the man while he slept.

Teachers probably find it frustrating when they're more memorable than the subject they're trying to teach. Hawthorne wrote a story we were supposed to learn from but then again Hawthorne had died, he was not part of our class, while Mr. Thomas had gray hair and a gray beard and he was tall and made specific requests of us. He asked us to do something different each day. Drive home from school on a different route or go about our morning routine in a different order. He asked us to look more closely into the mirror, we were supposed to stare into the mirror for a long time and try to see one thing about ourselves we had never seen before, and when he asked for a report about our experience with the mirror Jesse explained that his suntan was fading because of the long winter and Aaron had found a weird mark on his neck and Mr. Thomas tilted his head, a smile-grimace, like he appreciated the attempt but that wasn't quite what he meant. I had forgotten to do the mirror thing at all.

Mr. Thomas once read to our class an essay he had written about hugging. The school administration had recently implemented a new policy restricting physical contact between teachers and students, and Mr. Thomas read this essay he wrote about how a hug could bring relief or comfort. How a hug could be very simple and very important. How some young people had no person in their whole lives who listened to them or supported them emotionally and sometimes teachers could be that person; for some students, sometimes, a hug could express that support. *I am here for you. I care that you are doing okay.* But now the school had barred physical contact and Mr. Thomas read to us about why he felt this decision was an error. It seemed deeply vulnerable for a man to stand in front of thirty teenagers and describe his sincere regret that he was not allowed to offer his support for our well-being in this way anymore, and maybe his essay sounds creepy and Mr. Thomas is coming off as a predator but that's sort of my point. He believed learning involved care, which sometimes involved human contact, and the delicateness, or hazardousness, of that position required a written form with some audacity. He needed a form that could explain itself by enacting its idea: an essay about an act of care could *be* that act of care. That was how it felt to listen. To me at least. It felt like being cared about.

. . . .

Mr. Thomas wrote comments in the margins about why I shouldn't begin sentences with *There are* or *There is* or *It was* or *It is*. His comments took something apart. Like I'd been looking at a clock and thinking, Okay so for a clock to work the hands must go in circles, and Mr. Thomas turned over the clock and removed the rear plate and said, Actually come see this, come see all this intricate stuff inside you're required to worry about. He always found my gears missing or the teeth not lined up right. He gave me a perfect score exactly once, on an essay about agnosticism.

I'd learned the word *agnosticism* earlier that year from a rogue Sunday school teacher named Dan. My high school Sunday school class was rambunctious, and we kept driving away our teachers until the church couldn't be picky anymore. Dan took us to breakfast at a restaurant called the Frontier, one block from the church. It felt transgressive to leave the church during church time, like we were playing hooky, but we did, we walked to the Frontier and sat at a long table in the back. On the wall hung a large painting of that same spot in the restaurant, but the painting featured a round table and around it sat thirteen old white people, mostly men, some in coveralls, some in hats, collared shirts tucked in, all of them drinking coffee, doing what they might call *visiting* or *fellowship*. A woman in the background refills the salad bar. We sat beneath the painting and ordered plates of eggs and bacon and Sam ordered steak, rare, and Dan laughed and said, You know it's going to come out bloody, and maybe Sam understood and maybe he didn't but he acted like he did and gobbled down his blood-steak.

Dan asked how our week had gone. That was how he always started. He asked what was going on in our lives. Once, Brad said he had driven thirty miles to Iowa City because Frito-Lay had a distribution facility there and they discarded all the expired chips into a bin outside and every month Brad filled the trunk of his car with expired chips which tasted fine, he said, and it was true they tasted fine, I knew because sometimes Brad shared his chips with the cross-country team after practice, he popped the trunk of his car and we snacked. Dan called Brad a dumpster diver and asked where the place was but Brad refused to say, the chip source was his secret, he wouldn't budge, and this was a time when you couldn't just look things up very easily so Dan said, Okay, I respect that. And I got the sense he really did. Respect it.

Dan let us paint our Sunday school room. He thought the space should belong to us, so he brought in paint and we drew concept art and began with a coat of white primer, four of us painting the walls, and soon I started to feel dizzy and warm and hilarious and so did Evan, everything was hysterical, too much so, and Dan looked at the can of paint and read the label and bent over his own gut laughing at the paint can, and later that afternoon the church custodian came into the gas station where I worked and complained to me that the damn high school kids had painted their classroom *with lead paint* and it was going to take a *month* to air out the church and I didn't tell him I was one of the damn high school kids or that we were painting the classroom because the church belonged to us, too, even if our acts of belonging were flawed.

What made Dan rogue, though, is that he asked if we believed in God. Really asked. We had already confirmed ourselves in the Methodist church.

We had memorized the books of the Bible and helped with church services and spent two weeks of summer at a cabin in the woods and sat around a fire at night and sang all the major-key hope music, and not just in a boring mandatory sing-along kind of way, we learned the songs and we each had favorites and preferences about them and on the very last night we sat around the fire and sang and cried and hugged each other and thrummed with joy and the joy came from the music but also from above the music somehow, or beyond it, I understood I was supposed to remember this moment around the fire as a moment of love and I was supposed to attribute this love to God because he invented it. But never during the process did anyone ask if I believed in God in a way that suggested I was supposed to think about the question carefully. The process was called *confirmation*; I understood I was *confirming*, not exploring. I should confirm the answer, like if the pastor had asked, What is the charge of an electron? How do you spell *phalanx*? What is the capital city of Maine? How much do you believe in God?

Dan talked with us about faith and spirituality, and these conversations would later cause the parents to become alarmed and cause Dan to be replaced and cause Sam's parents to become the new teachers and gather us in a circle in a different classroom and in a remedial tone Sam's mom would say we understand many of you have decided you don't believe in God and this makes us deeply worried and frustrated. Dan had asked how we felt. He tried to offer guidance. I don't know, Evan had said. Maybe there is a god but maybe there isn't. How am I supposed to know? I don't know. How is anyone supposed to know for sure? And Dan said, It sounds like you're an agnostic. That's something you can be. You can be unsure if you want. You don't have to be sure. That's called being an agnostic.

Earlier in the conversation I had said I didn't think God was real, and Kristen had agreed that God wasn't real, we were both going to be atheists, but I liked this new category and said actually I'm not sure about God either. I switched to Evan's category. Kristen stayed an atheist. Wesley stayed a Methodist. Brad said he didn't know if he believed in God totally but the way he didn't know was different from the way Evan didn't know, like he was not *set* about his uncertainty, if that makes sense, he could still become certain one way or the other. It was the realest conversation about faith I'd ever been a part of and when later the adults admonished us for having it I knew I couldn't go to church anymore, and when later Mom asked if I was going to church that week and I said no, I didn't want to anymore, and she asked *at all*, and I said yes *at all* and she cried, all I meant was: *I'm not sure who, if anyone, designed the universe and I'm not sure who, if anyone, is managing it presently.*

And like, no kidding.

And like, I understand many versions of faith allow for mesmerizing uncertainty, allow for mystery, even require mystery, center mystery, but I got a different version where God was a fact, and God was the source of the river of facts, he was the headwaters all facts flowed from, and sometimes the river of facts was cold and painful and the pain was confusing but it was no less a river of facts and the facts no less began with him, so you could express sorrow or joy about the river but you couldn't ask questions about where the current came from because that issue had already been resolved forever, is the version I got.

Sometimes I wonder how often the misbehaved teacher never enters the room. What if we had driven away fewer of Dan's predecessors and he never had to show up? How many questions hung in a room unspoken because an adult wanted to avoid pissing off an administrator? How often did the misbehaved teacher never enter the room, and how often did the misbehaved teacher live inside the behaved one, collaborating, feeding them lines, making sure they didn't get replaced by Sam's parents while smuggling ideas into the room in a way maybe the young people might not even understand? Something almost subtle like, Your routine is also a rule system. You can do better at looking into the mirror. You can do better at seeing yourself. You are not choosing the words you are saying. You are following your intuition. An intuition is also a rule system. An intuition is a subgenre of certainty and the radical thing to do is effort. Effort of diction. Effort of syntax. Look into the mirror with effort, travel home with effort, begin the sentence with effort, and what the effort brings you closer to might be yourself and it might be each other.

Once, Dan asked how our week had gone and Wesley reported that what he did during the week was rewrite the lyrics to a popular hip-hop song so the song was no longer about sex, it was now about eating breadsticks, it was a praise song about breadsticks. Wesley was the most timid of the class. He had a small body and a goofy smile. He liked to sink into a bean-bag chair in the corner, chin down, looking up over his glasses. When he told us about the breadsticks song, he looked proudly conspiratorial, like his body contained 14,000 secrets and this song was the tip of the iceberg of secrets. Dan said, *Please* sing the whole thing for us, and Wesley did. Magnificently. And I felt I knew him better, felt closer to him, like here is this creative weirdo rapping in the church basement about breadsticks. This is what he carries around. This is how the world sieves through his weird brain. Dork recognize dork.

Effort had made it possible to arrive here. An effort of pedagogy. An effort of connection. No one else could have gotten Wesley to sit up in the beanbag chair and rap about breadsticks, but Dan created a space that praised our differences, our doubt, our variously conflicted efforts at belief and Wesley accepted the space, he performed in it, then fell back into his seat with a grin, a smirk, his arms crossed.

Distance from the Question, or Notes on Being Asked about a War

In the first scene of the pilot episode of the sitcom *One Day at a Time*, Penelope, a nurse, gives a routine physical to a man in an orange plaid shirt and blue jeans; he has a mustache and thick-rimmed glasses. She holds a clipboard to her chest. Taped to the back of the clipboard is a photo of three women in military uniforms. The man sees the photo and assumes the women are dressing up for Halloween. Penelope smiles and says no, not Halloween, the photo was taken closer to Christmas. "But you're wearing army clothes," he says. Penelope, still smiling: "Yes, the camouflage look was all the rage in Afghanistan." The man catches on. She is an army veteran. He says: "Let me ask you—" but Penelope cuts him off: "No, I never killed anyone, yes it was hot over there, you're welcome for my service, anything else?"

It turns out his question was actually about her husband: "I was going to ask if your husband is also a badass soldier." It turns out the man on the exam room table does not care if Penelope killed anyone or if it was hot over there. He's flirting, trying to determine her relationship status. But his flirting allows for an oblique sort of learning. We learn Penelope has been asked certain questions before. We learn that public understanding of the war centers on death and heat and gratitude for having tolerated death and heat—that a lot of people ask apparently superficial questions about Penelope's former life and that she finds these questions tedious. War comes into the room via questions no one in the room has asked. Which makes me wonder: Upon seeing the photo, what is the question he should've asked? When Penelope taped the photo to her clipboard, what is the question she hoped for?

People have asked me if I saw any action, and what was it like, and if it was hot over there. My aunt's church friend asked me, What was the strangest thing you ever saw in Afghanistan? We were hiking a mountain in Oregon, walking in a row. They were up front because it was their first time on the trail, and I wanted them to feel like they were leading the way into this beautiful place. I thought about the question. I didn't know how to include in my answer any amount of respect for the people of Afghanistan, considering how much strangeness in a war zone is a response to cruelty. People act strangely when their homes are destroyed, when they are forced out of their communities, when they are afraid, when they are terrified, when they are despairing. Or not even *strangely*—they acted in ways that were unfamiliar to me but reasonable considering the circumstance. Strange on what scale? Strange compared to what? *Strange* subverts an expectation. *Strange* is exceptional. Not what it was like most of the time, but the exception to what it was like. Not routine, but novel. The strangest thing you saw during a war—this will be an anecdote about disorder amid disorder, an anecdote that will have to be trafficked between the guardrails of appropriateness: You will still have to say the thing out loud. To your aunt's friend from church. In that moment on the trail, I didn't answer, because I didn't understand what exactly she meant. I let the conversation continue to something else.

In retrospect, probably the strangest thing I ever saw in Afghanistan was the presence of American troops there, including myself, nine years after the war started.

. . . .

In the story collection *Redeployment*, Phil Klay puts two veterans in a bar and makes them talk to a well-meaning liberal who wants to know about the war, about "what's really going on," so she can help other veterans do creative writing about their experience. In another of Klay's stories, a veteran is on the Amherst campus and confronts a student who wants to know "the real scoop on what was going on." They sit on the veteran's porch and smoke a hookah, and the veteran tells war stories in the hope of bridging what tends to be called the civilian-military divide.

In Steven Kiernan's short story "The Difference between Us," the narrator is at a bar in San Francisco when he is asked about Iraq: "What's the worst thing you saw over there?" The narrator tells a story that happened in North Carolina. The narrator's platoon is supposed to be helping survivors of Hurricane Katrina by bringing them furniture and supplies from garrison. But instead of hauling the things in an orderly way down to the trucks, the marines start throwing bunks from the second story. They start destroying every single thing they are supposed to give to the people who are hurting. In the bar, the narrator's audience does not understand the point of the story. She asks him to tell another.

In her essay about returning from deployment, Lizbeth Prifogle turns these moments into a composite. The civilian is a plurality. The moment is a summary of moments, where she is asked, How was it over there? Are you going back? How hot was it? And so on. Prifogle responds in acronyms, meaning to confuse the civilian, meaning to "boggle their civilian brains." She is toying with them. She says yeah, maybe she wants to go back. Maybe to Afghanistan. She wants to seem a little "crazy," but she also wants to make the point that she is a marine and this is her job, and pitying someone for doing the job they volunteered to do is ridiculous. She admits the temperature reached 110 degrees at 20:00 hours. She frames the extreme within the ordinary—the radical heat in early evening, the evening counted on a system maybe you don't understand, all of it a matter of routine. She normalizes. She is a person going to work. How was work? It was fine. She is going back tomorrow, same as you.

In his book *The Forever War*, the reporter Dexter Filkins describes encountering the divide like this, in Cambridge:

People asked me about the war, of course. They asked me whether it was as bad as people said. "Oh definitely," I told them, and then, usually, I stopped. In the beginning I'd go on a little longer, tell them a story or two, and I could see their eyes go after a couple of sentences. We drew closer to each other, the hacks and the vets and the diplomats, anyone who'd been over there. My friend George, an American reporter I'd gotten to know in Iraq, told me he couldn't have a conversation with anyone about Iraq who hadn't been there. I told him I couldn't have a conversation with anyone who hadn't been there about anything at all.

For a writer to admit this is remarkable. Filkins is reporting for the *New York Times*. His friend George is George Packer of the *New Yorker*. Their job is to hold difficult conversations with the American public about things for which the American public is responsible. Their job is to inform us. In person, they find this impossible. The only people they can talk to are the people who *already understand* what they understand. The people who hadn't been there are the ones most in need of this experience, and some are asking, *Are things as bad as I've heard?* They, too, are trying to draw closer. Filkins writes, *I could see their eyes go.* What does that mean? They are bored? Horrified? Stunned? Fatigued? Disinterested? Why? Whose fault is that?

I'm attracted to these moments because I feel caught between them. I deployed to Afghanistan but not Iraq. I wore a uniform for a short period—on and off for seven years. I know some of the language. I share some of the stories, but there is a lot I don't understand. I have a lot of tactless curiosity. Some of the questions I have are discourteous. Deployments can be so different. Did you have the kind of deployment where you lived in a hole, or did you have the kind with air conditioning and running water and wireless internet? Mine was both, depending on the month. I want to know if you laugh about it. Do you hate it? Are you furious or regretful or indifferent or both or neither? Lately though, I want to know what compels the writer to take the civilian's question and put it on the page. I wonder if the writer does this because the question is bad, and they want to convey the badness to their audience—look at what badness I'm confronted with sometimes—to warn people away from acting like that. I wonder if sometimes the question is sincerely compelling. If these questions are the only openings people have to think about their experience. A slight crack in the everyday, into which the writer can slip their fingers and pull.

. . . .

Elliot Ackerman, a former lieutenant, wrote about his experience leading a platoon in Iraq. His essay "A Battle in Falluja, Revisited" uses the narrative contained in the documentation for his Silver Star. The official story is a scaffold; Ackerman splits apart the paragraphs in order to augment them

Distance from the Question

with his own memory. In one section, Ackerman describes calling for indirect fire on twenty-five enemy fighters:

> They were just standing at a bend in the road. They were all wearing black. I took my time calling in the mortars, but because they were at a bend in the road I knew exactly where they were. I whispered the grid coordinates into the radio and then I waited. They just disappeared when the rounds impacted. After a couple of minutes a gentle breeze cleared up the smoke. It looked like someone had dumped a pile of wet black rags in the road.

The next paragraph jumps forward in time:

> When I come home, more often than you might expect, a stranger will ask me if I ever killed anyone. For a long time, I didn't know how to answer that question. A friend of mine took to saying, "If I did, you paid me to," which eventually I also took to saying, but the first person who asks me is my cousin, and she is 6 years old.

The writing moves from the official account, to his memory of the call-for-fire, to the way the moment reverberates years later. We don't learn what Ackerman said to his cousin. During the time when he didn't know how to answer the question about killing, we don't learn what he said instead. We learn he borrowed a response, which itself is not definitive—*If I did*—but instead seeks to redistribute the moral fault of killing, from individual to public, which proves useless when he is confronted by a six-year-old who does not pay federal taxes and is not morally complicit in Ackerman's experience in combat.

Ackerman's rendering of the moment itself is violent but muted, literally and otherwise. He is patient and deliberate. He whispers the coordinates over the radio. The fighters don't explode; they disappear. The shapes of their bodies become a pile of tattered clothes on the street. Later, he describes assaulting a room with other marines, two of whom have been shot. The house where they are fighting is on fire. There is smoke and dust. The immediate presence of the enemy is rendered with more attention to soft noise: "I can hear them inside, speaking in gasps, shuffling through the debris, as slowly—grenade by grenade and bullet by bullet—we kill them." The syntax is methodical, to match the rate of death. *As slowly we kill them* is a formal way of putting it, further interrupted with the phrase *grenade by grenade and bullet by bullet*, which suggests the amount and degree of violence in a way that mutes its spectacle.

Technically, these moments answer a question—if he ever killed anyone—but the answer and the question are each less important than the answer's distance *from* the question. Something separates his response from the inquiry that provokes it, and that separation represents all the things Ackerman believes his audience will not understand about the literal yes or no. His answer doesn't just need to transmit the information; he has to get that stranger from the place of their asking to the place of his response. He has to traverse the distance between those places. This is a hard thing to do in person. But his written account—its syntax and grammar and tone—responds to the distance. He is trying to cover some ground.

Did you kill anyone? is morbid curiosity. The desire, perhaps, to hear intimate details about some of the more grisly circumstances human beings inflict on each other. If this instinct is driving the strangers' question—if their curiosity about killing is a kind of yearning—Ackerman has a problem, because his story contains a lot of what these strangers yearn for. He seems uncomfortable fulfilling that desire. In the story, he reminds us of the quietude. The whispering of the fighters' location into the radio. Their vanishing: "They just disappeared when the rounds impacted." Syntactically, the fighters are dead *before* the mortars hit. The fighters disappear and then we learn how, which erases the drama of the mortars' falling arc. The verb for the killing is similarly undramatic—*impacted*—a verb the *American Heritage Dictionary* describes as ranking "among the most detested of English usage." The dictionary note can't explain why the usage panel dislikes *impacted* so much—"even the literal use of the verb was found unacceptable by a majority"—and I wonder if the word simply doesn't connote the violence it describes. It sounds administrative. But here the tonal wrongness of the word is appropriate. It creates a dissonance.

This dissonance is what I mean by the answer's distance from the question. The smoke is gone before we learn it exists: "After a couple of minutes a gentle breeze cleared up the smoke." The violence is whispering and waiting followed by disappearance and a breeze. The passage is tonally quiet, *gentle*, even fleeting, until it isn't. By contrast, the tattered clothes of the dead men are heavy and mutilated. All of this answers a question Ackerman hasn't yet put on the page. *If I killed anyone*: He gives us the answer first in order to reconstruct the meaning of *kill*, which here is the process of whispering and impacting, followed by the meaning of *I*, which here is the person waiting and observing, followed by the meaning of *anyone*, which here is twenty-five men at a bend in the road. By the time the question appears—*if I killed anyone*—he has redefined all of its terms. We see their meaning closer to the way Ackerman does, while understanding, too, the position of the stranger who asked. We see the question both ways, and the distance from the one to the other is extraordinary.

Maybe this distance, from the question to its answer, is one way to measure discourtesy.

Maybe this distance is one way to measure the impolite.

Maybe the only thing wrong with such questions is how the person answering them has to cover some ground on their way to the answer, and asking a person to cover this particular ground is asking kind of a lot for the sake of your curiosity.

. . . .

In their essay "Letters to My Country That She Will Never Read," Drew Pham is at a party with other writers, and the writers are talking about war, which means they are talking about books about war, including Klay's *Redeployment*. Pham notes how writers love its opening sentence, "We shot dogs." But Pham believes something is missing in the story that follows that sentence, and in the essay they offer their own story to supplement the record. Pham and his buddies also shot dogs, but the killing was different from what Klay describes. Less redeemable. Less about mercy. The killing is an act of either desire or derangement or both. The undertow here is self-destruction. Pham describes how the stress of being in Afghanistan turns fast into madness, "the kind of madness that makes you an animal," and then Pham writes about killing an animal. I wonder if Klay's book helped in that moment at the party. Like maybe the book taught some civilians that sometimes soldiers kill dogs, which then put Pham in the position of needing to distinguish between *reasons* for killing dogs. Like maybe the literature has gotten the civilians up to speed a bit. Instead of starting from *Did you kill anyone?* they were starting from *Did you kill any dogs?* which is closer to a certain sort of truth. Like the conversation must periodically rise up out of the book, then go back in.

. . . .

These encounters with the divide often take place in literary or academic settings. For instance, Hugh Martin's poem "The War Was Good, Thank You" is a response to a question he is asked on a college campus. Maybe former soldiers are disproportionately interested in art and academia. Maybe they are just flush with money from the GI Bill, so they keep ending up in these situations. Maybe the insularity of a college campus serves as a neat counterpoint to the insularity of military culture. Maybe it's a good sign. A campus is supposed to be an environment where people ask difficult questions about serious matters of geopolitics. Each encounter is a dialectic.

In *Unbecoming: A Memoir of Disobedience*, Anuradha Bhagwati has recently separated from the marines and finds herself writing a paper on American torture policy for a renowned Harvard professor. The professor has recently announced his support for the war in Iraq, drawing the ire of progressives, and has now presented his students with an image from Abu Ghraib, asking them if it qualifies as torture, apparently in an effort to provoke his progressive students to an opinion that he will then *complicate* or *trouble*. Bhagwati doesn't take the bait in that direction: "Some folks dismissed the exercise immediately, calling my professor a war criminal behind his back. But I lived in the no-man's-land between right and wrong. I felt compelled to undergo the intellectual exercise of examining what I believed and formulating a new worldview, a handbook, on morality. I wasn't going to swallow the ethical guidelines of a fairy-tale universe, where people were conveniently marked as either heroes or villains."

She decides to write favorably about torture, and a "pacifist" friend approaches her and asks about the writing. Bhagwati describes her own willingness to commit violence in the right circumstances. She tells her friend, "I'd remove fingernails, then hack off fingers, one by one." Her friend tells her "that's fucked up." Bhagwati reflects and realizes it is.

What intrigues me about this encounter with the divide is how Bhagwati doesn't see herself across a distance but stuck in the middle of one. Even though she recounts her position firmly and describes her inclination to violence—she calls it "lust"—Bhagwati still imagines herself in a middle space, in a "no-man's-land." She's not on the right while the pacifist is on the left. She doesn't agree, necessarily, with the professor. Her attitude toward violence feels different. More complicated. She writes, "Folks at Harvard seemed like phantoms of a force-fed childhood, where you simply believed what you were told to believe." She implicates herself as a phantom of another institution, a phantom of marine violence, except the beliefs she adopted from that institution aren't as "simple" as the beliefs of the academic. Not a matter of heroes and villains. Like she's operating on a different scale where violence is just the hard thing to do. The difficult, grown-up thing. This posture soon reveals its more cynical core. The pacifist calls her lust "fucked up" and she agrees, writing, "There was no pride in this moment. Just a sick realization of what and who I had become." *Unbecoming* refers, of course, not just to disobedience but to the reconstruction of identity.

. . . .

In 2009, I attended a reading at the Englert Theatre in Iowa City. The essayist John D'Agata was introducing John McPhee, and in the introduction D'Agata quoted Goethe: "Experience is only half of experience." I was an undergraduate sitting in the balcony, taking notes in the dark. I scrawled down this quotation verbatim but neglected to include its source, so for twelve years I thought the statement was D'Agata's own, maybe an early version of his challenge against veracity. Or maybe a way to dethrone personal experience by championing history and context. Experience is only half. There is also whatever brought you to the experience. Whatever surrounds it. Whatever helped form its meaning. I didn't know the idea came from German poetry; I thought D'Agata was just being grumpy about traditionally scenic, narrative literature. I like the idea as a challenge, as a test against the way meaning is formed in the past and present. To put it in the context of war: a question about the experience of war is only half about the experience of war. The question should be about the total breadth of military culture, but it's often reduced to being about war only. A story about the civilian-military divide is an encounter with that reduction. Like if you were asked to explain the function of a lamp by discussing only the glass of its bulb. To say nothing of the electricity.

In a story about the civilian-military divide, the characters are often crossing many divides at once. Civilian-military scholars have identified at least nine different gaps influenced by military experience—gaps related to political ideology, personal values, geography, sacrifice, and familiarity with military culture and language, among others. It's true a service member may have witnessed something horrific during a war, and what they witnessed could make them feel separated from the broader American public. They may also feel separated because they use a separate health-care system, or because they know a separate vocabulary, or because they lived in military-centric communities like Columbus, Georgia, or Twentynine Palms, California, or because their service has given them a different perspective on how government should work and why sometimes it doesn't.

I've lived most of my life in Iowa and Oregon, neither of which is home to any significant military installations. Growing up, I never thought of this as an absence, because I never experienced it as a presence. I thought I was familiar enough with the military because the town where I grew up had National Guard and Reserve units. But gathering your understanding of the military this way is like believing you know what it means to live in a university town because nearby there is a community college. One supplements the community; the other transforms it. Like universities, military bases bring huge populations of transient young people, an influx of jobs, and economic dependence on a single industry. The young people live together in cramped spaces. They are by turns miserable and inspired. Their immaturity can lead to violence. The violence committed by these young people can be extraordinary. In Karie Fugett's essay "Unusual Objects," she describes the landscape outside Camp Lejeune this way:

> Jacksonville [North Carolina] was a man's world, the whole damn place a bachelor pad. The main road leading to Camp Lejeune wasn't much more than asphalt and spindly pines. The rest was car lots, strip clubs, and tattoo parlors, chain restaurants, and a sad excuse for a mall. Young men with matching crew cuts roamed in packs on the sides of roads. Colorful hot rods purchased with deployment money revved up at red lights. . . . Background noise was artillery rounds and low-flying aircraft, both so loud they often set off car alarms. Few people were local, nearly all its residents transplants somehow connected to the Marine Corps.

In Jacksonville, it is safe to assume every person you meet has some connection to the military. The military is how an eighteen-year-old kid bought a sports car, and the military is where he drives it. The military is background and foreground, road and weeds and earth and every business for sixty miles. The military roams the roadside in packs. It sets off car alarms without touching the cars; the military is both the cause of the shock wave and the oxygen it moves through.

I try to imagine entering this world for the first time.

I try to imagine *leaving* this world for the first time.

* *

The difficulty of imagining such a world arises, in part, because American military culture tends to be so geographically concentrated. Certain regions of the country are more fluent than others. Most Georgians know more about it than most Iowans. Southern California is more dependent on the military economy than Idaho or Montana. Once, at a work conference in Baltimore, I met a North Carolina woman who during the long round of formal introductions stood and introduced herself to the room as being from Cumberland County, North Carolina, "home of the All-Americans." I looked around the room for expressions of recognition but couldn't find any. People had come to the conference from all over the country—I met attendees from the Virgin Islands, Massachusetts, Michigan, Florida, Colorado—but when she named the All-Americans I saw no nods, no signals anyone knew what she meant, that the 82nd Airborne Division, nicknamed the All-Americans, is stationed at Fort Bragg, just outside of Fayetteville. In the broader military culture, the nickname of the 82nd isn't esoteric knowledge. Nor is it esoteric in Cumberland County. But the civilian-military divide is geographic that way. Military culture is partly an expression of regional culture, and vice versa.

Maybe for this reason, stories about encountering the divide often occur in hubs like cities and university towns, places that converge experience from a broad swath. Amherst, Cambridge, San Francisco. Places, too, that serve as ripe settings for tension because they signal a more liberal demographic, as well as an intellectual or artistic class. Klay references the theater scene of New York City. Pham is hanging out with writers. These narrators are crossing gaps of political ideology, geography, and varying sorts of labor, all at once. Kiernan's narrator is in San Francisco, being asked about the worst thing he saw in Iraq, and responding with a story set in North Carolina. Klay's narrator is in Amherst, trying to explain Iraq by way of his childhood in northern Virginia. What matters as much as the place where a person deployed is the place where they came from and the place they returned to. If you feel concerned about young men with matching crew cuts roaming the roadsides of a place you have never been, maybe the story you need to hear is not about Iraq or Afghanistan. Maybe it is about Jacksonville.

Filkins, again: "Back in the world, there was a kind of underground conversation about Iraq and Afghanistan. Underground and underclass. The rest of the country didn't much care. In Pearland and Osawatomie and LaGrange, Iraq and Afghanistan lived on, and people wanted to talk. I think they liked talking to me because I wasn't one of them; I came from Cambridge, not Osawatomie. They were tired of talking to each other. I was tired of talking to myself."

What the towns of Pearland and Osawatomie and LaGrange have in common is loss. Earlier in *The Forever War* a young man from Pearland, Texas, is killed on a mission that Filkins and his photographer take part in. The death is especially difficult because it seems, at least initially, that documenting the war has worsened it, that the man died because the photographer wanted to get a very particular photograph, which required the platoon to take a certain action, which led them into gunfire, which killed the man from Pearland, Texas. Filkins, to remind us of his own distance from the marines he is reporting about, initially mistakes the name of the town as a reference to pearls instead of pears.

Loss refocuses the war. Some scholars would call this the Sacrifice Gap. The gap between who is suffering the destruction of life and who is not. Filkins describes the conversation around this gap as *underground*, implying both urgency and illicitness—something that should not be talked about in daylight but still must be talked about. The conversation is underground, presumably, because the rest of the country is not just indifferent but so aggressively indifferent that it hampers the dialogue, forces it below the surface, where it remains small and insulate, and thus tired. Osawatomie is a town of less than 5,000 people, forty miles southwest of Kansas City, and I get the sense that Filkins references these places as if to remind his reader they exist. He calls this "back in the world" as if Iraq and Afghanistan are outside of civilization, but he also seems to suggest that these towns, too, are hanging onto the world by a thread. These are places where the wars "lived on" as if, in fact, the wars had ended and these towns were stuck in time. As if the instinct to discuss wars that are ongoing is somehow quaint or outdated.

For Filkins, the divide, too, is economic. Those who are talking about the war are "underclass," which implies that those who are not talking about the war, those who "didn't much care," have some money. As of this writing, one bonus available for enlisting into the military is $70,000. How a person responds to the possibility of $70,000 says a lot about their relationship to finances. For some, no amount of money *on earth* could make them do something like that, while some might simply re-emphasize it's $70,000.

Me, I bought a car after basic training, after I received the first half of a $10,000 signing bonus. I got a reenlistment bonus six years later, along with a monthly pay increase, as an incentive to extend my contract by one year so I would deploy to Afghanistan. Tuition assistance and the GI Bill helped me avoid the paralyzing debt that has become a defining characteristic of my generation. I don't think anyone should have to do any of this. I hardly recommend it. But you can imagine why some, in part, do.

In high school there was also a big incentive to persuade your friends to enlist. Or the incentive felt big at the time. For each "lead to enlistment" you provided to a recruiter, you received $2,000—$1,000 when the recruit signed the paperwork and $1,000 when they shipped to basic training. A lot of people I knew were signing up. I don't think anyone was persuading anyone else to join, but we submitted the lead forms to get the bonus money, then split the money with the person who was enlisting, 75–25 because the forms were a pain in the ass. Eventually this program would be shut down due to widespread fraud involving more than a thousand people, from high school kids to recruiters to colonels to generals. Recruiters were submitting leads for their own recruits, or sharing in the profit of their own leads, or sharing with a superior officer, or sharing with a friend. In total, the program paid out more than $300 million, a third of which was officially determined to be fraudulent.

Before the story broke, about the corruption of recruiters and generals and seventeen-year-olds, here is how my senior year of high school went: Gary enlisted first, as a radio operator, because Gary was color blind and this was one of the few specialties the army allowed him. Gary submitted the lead form for Tony, who enlisted in the same unit. Gary and Tony were best friends, so maybe Gary convinced Tony that the military was a good idea, or maybe they grew up in the same place under similar persuasions, but either way Gary and Tony split the money from the lead and purchased body kits for their Pontiacs. They had recently seen *The Fast and the Furious* and chose to adopt its culture for themselves, which meant they parked their cars along the main drag in town—called the Four Lanes because it was the only road in town with so many lanes—and let the blue lights from the underbodies of their cars shine onto the pavement, hip-hop blaring from the stereos in the trunk. Gary submitted the lead for me. Tony submitted the lead for Rick, who enlisted as a combat engineer. Rick ran distance on my track team, and the only time I saw him after graduation was during pre-mobilization training for Afghanistan when, during a convoy exercise, my Humvee fake-exploded and black dirt rushed past my window, and as it cleared Rick strode past, emerging from the dirt cloud and then disappearing into it again. I guess engineers sometimes helped with the fake explosives. He didn't see me. I don't know how he spent his part of the money.

I submitted the lead for Kurt, who rode the same bus as me through elementary school. In high school, Kurt started wearing tight-fitting shirts to accentuate his muscles, which he worked on all the time at the gym on the town square. The culture Kurt chose for himself was fighting. Mixed martial arts. At first, Fight Night happened above that gym on the town square, every Sunday night, until the event became a liability for the business and moved to the National Guard armory. Fighting was a liability for the armory too, but the recruiter, Sergeant Webber, didn't care. He liked the foot traffic. I never learned if Kurt was a good fighter. I only went to Fight Night once, because I heard Gary would be fighting, and I wanted to see someone kick his ass, which they did. A lot of guys at my high school thought they were good at fighting because Sergeant Webber visited our gym class every year to teach us the basic parts of the army's fighting techniques, trying to recruit us during our mandatory classes, which I guess no one felt was strange. So then guys showed up to Fight Night and punched each other. Maybe Kurt was a great fighter. Maybe he was a genius. I forget what job he enlisted to do, but when the money came through from his lead-to-enlistment, I drove to the ATM at the motor bank, withdrew $500, and parked in front of the gym on the town square. I put the cash in an envelope that I had brought along for that purpose and walked into the gym and handed him the envelope and he nodded at me like we were two sly motherfuckers, and a few weeks later he came to school bearing the results of the cash, which was a half-sleeve tattoo, on his bulging left forearm, of a poorly inked American flag.

Of Prerogative!

. . . .

I learned the word *latigo* from a Garth Brooks song about a cowboy following his dream. In the song, Garth is cataloging things you might see at a
rodeo: Animals. Hats. Boots. Blood. Audience. Rope. Steers. Latigo. A latigo
is the leather strap affixing the cowboy's hand to the bull. The song is really
about passion; the lyrics figure rodeo as an Other Woman seducing the
cowboy away from his relationship. Rodeo, for him, is both a source of joy
and a source of grief. It is also an untenable career choice. The cowboy tries
to make his passion produce money for him, but ruin is poised over him
all the time. Ruin raises the stakes. It makes him a loner, which is to say it
makes him an artist. The latigo cinches his hand to an animal that wants
nothing to do with him, and his dream is to never get free.

I learned the word *centrifugal* from a Faith Hill song about kissing. A
song also about passion. Faith describes kissing using the language of New-
tonian mechanics because the standard vocabulary for passion—words like
bliss, for example—are not syllabic enough for the spectacular happiness
they represent. Like how *sun* compares so meekly to its referent.

I learned *prerogative* from Shania Twain's "Man! I Feel Like a Woman!,"
the first single from her 1997 hit record *Come On Over*. Shania sings about
prerogative as a kind of personal agency, an agency that connects immediately with joy. For Shania, the main thing to do with agency is move toward happiness, a movement the song codes as feminine—and moreover,
ultimately feminine. Women, more than anything else, are empowered to

pursue fun. She sounds like she's having fun even as she sings it. I have fun when I listen, even now. I have been listening to it a lot lately.

. . . .

As a kid, I learned from country music. I owned cassette tapes of Alan Jackson, Tim McGraw, Billy Ray Cyrus, and Bryan White, as well as Garth and Shania. I owned a compilation of country songs called *Farther Down the Road*, a promotional product released by the Shell Oil Company that included, between each song, a commercial for Shell Rotella motor oil. The album artwork featured an armadillo crossing a rural highway beset by flat land and blue sky, an image that had been manipulated to exaggerate the curvature of the earth. The bands of the armadillo's armor had been manipulated to resemble piano keys. On the compilation, George Strait's narrator responds to heartbreak by driving to a rodeo in Wyoming. Tracy Byrd offers his love by comparing it to Wyoming. His love is a wide, open space. His love is a wilderness area. His love has a gigantic sky and zero fences. The way he describes it, you get the sense his love is technically operated by the Bureau of Land Management but he wants you to believe it is untended. Pure. The vast acreage of his love also means freedom.

In country music, place mattered a lot.

Location rarely stayed ambiguous.

Alan Jackson sang about summer in Georgia.

Pam Tillis sang about summer in Memphis.

Garth Brooks sang about a hookup in Baton Rouge.

The band Alabama sang about you can probably guess which place.

I lived in Iowa. The only song I remember that mentioned Iowa was Jo Dee Messina's "Heads Carolina, Tails California," about a narrator and her companion escaping, for once, some unnamed place. They are trying to get out. They are brainstorming where to go. They are naming off places. How about Boston. How about Des Moines. The song is about love, chance, discovery, mountains, the automatic heroism of distance. The song is about a coin flip, which leads me to think the lyrics reference the greater Des Moines metro area only because the pre-chorus needed to rhyme the word *coin*.

You get the sense the coin will land on tails.

You get the sense the lovers will not be making their great escape to central Iowa.

The story was never about us. Country songs mythologized experiences in the South and the western plains, which, as heard by midwesterners, became a triple-jump of narrative fantasy: made-up stories about an invented version of a place that never belonged to us anyway.

I didn't understand any of this at the time and let me give you an example of how much I didn't understand.

Once, when I was eight or nine, I watched a VHS tape of a Garth Brooks live performance and felt so compelled by his energy onstage that I smashed my toy guitar over the corner of a desk. Just like how Garth smashed his, the shattered body of the instrument dangling from its neck by strings, which prompted Mom to explain in no uncertain terms how Garth could *afford* lots of guitars, he had a whole *busload* of guitars, when Garth smashed a guitar someone just walked up and handed him a new one, and that was *not* how it worked in our house. Mom reminded me that yes, sometimes Garth's songs made it seem like he didn't have a lot of money, but he was an *entertainer*. He was pretending.

You do not really break the guitar.

You do not really drive to a rodeo in Wyoming.

You do not really use a coin to make important life decisions.

You put the coin into a jar until you are ready to spend it on muffin mix or ethanol.

You put the coin into a jar where its saved potential expands into a moral system.

. . . .

Place mattered a lot, but it was confusing. I once told my preschool teacher I lived on a farm, so she asked what kind of animals we raised, and I explained that my family had two dogs, two inside cats, five outside cats, and seven toads in the basement, so then she asked what crops we grew, and I said we grew tomatoes and green beans in the garden, so then she told me I didn't live on a farm, even though she'd never even been there.

Where I lived was the edge between country and town, which meant the country kids believed I was a town kid and the town kids believed I was a country kid and probably it's a myth that some people experience belonging but what I'm saying is I grew up on two acres of land within the city limits but down a gravel road amid cornfields. We drank city water but the newspaper arrived a day late. Technically, the land was an industrial park. A long brown factory loomed to our north. The previous owners of our property had sold live bait from a trough in the barn. The barn had recently collapsed during an especially violent windstorm, but the concrete trough remained where the barn used to be. Dad's old motorcycle leaned against it. We hadn't used the barn for much.

I don't know the word for this kind of place.

I understand the word is not *farm.*

. . . .

Sometimes I knew what a word meant but not within a certain context. I knew the word *independence* before Martina McBride released "Independence Day" in 1994, when I was seven, but I'm sure I didn't grasp the story, which means the story, to me, must have emerged. Like the song shapeshifted within my thinking. Maybe verse by verse, or line by line, or all at once, but somehow the song transformed into itself, a story about cruelty and violence and desperation and escape, and *independence* in this case meant a woman had burned her home to the ground with her abusive husband inside. The song is narrated by their daughter, orphaned after the fire. The man is presumably dead, the woman presumably in prison. Independence, in the song, forms against the contours of male brutality, against the kind of American masculinity that essayist Lacy Johnson rightly describes as terrorism. Which means the liberty is not really liberty at all, and not just because the woman goes to prison but because the masculinity she reacts against is so common, so indefatigable. So infinitely requiring of struggle.

Till then, *independence* had meant something different.

Independence had implied the historical.

Independence from the tyrannical kings of the past.

Independence from the fussy red-clothed army.

It had meant a violence sanitized by time.

It had meant less.

Once in fourth grade music class, the teacher asked us to bring a compact disc or cassette tape with a song we liked so she could play the songs one at a time while we sat in rows of blue plastic chairs facing forward listening. I remember this was supposed to be a reward for something, that we were allowed to spend time in music class listening to music we enjoyed. The song I brought was "That Summer" by Garth Brooks and I was excited to share it with my peers but when Mrs. Hanson played the song no one listened. The kids talked over it. The repetition of songs had bored them and the boredom had distracted them and Mrs. Hanson tried to shush the class but they kept chattering.

Of Prerogative!

It was probably for the best. What I didn't understand about the song was most of it. I knew the song was about desire and discovery, but I didn't know it was about, in particular, the statutory rape of a teenager by a much older woman. The song's narrator is a virgin who goes to work one summer on a farm where a widow lives alone. The age of the narrator is ambiguous. We know he is teenage. The word *kid* is used once. The word *boy* is used often. His exact distance from agency is unclear, and this is something you would allow to remain unclear only if clarity would get you in trouble.

The song's metaphors are straightforward: storms, comets, candles, hunger.

The storm is sex. The comet is sex. The hunger is for sex.

The candle is burning at both ends for these reasons.

The way Garth talks about the farm where they meet, you get the sense it is beyond civilization. Fields extend to the horizon. Fields extend through the horizon. The fields are boundless. This seems now like an important exaggeration. We are supposed to think the characters are beyond rules, beyond judgment. The vastness of rural America precipitates their aloneness while insulating them from moral scrutiny. But the vastness also creates a perilous balance of opportunity and threat: They are beyond judgment and they are beyond safety or rescue. They are beyond the law, which is either an intrusive stricture or a useful system of preventing harm. Either way, the boy is learning and the woman is unaccountable and this is fine because it is summer, which is the season of voyage.

Teenage desire involving farmworkers would reappear in country music. Garth Brooks released "That Summer" in 1993 and Deana Carter followed with "Strawberry Wine" in 1996, featuring a narrator whose grandfather employs a farmworker with whom the narrator begins a romantic relationship. At first, the narrator tells us that she was neither an adult nor a child, which is an odd way of saying she was seventeen, as we learn in the chorus. The distance between adulthood and childhood contains a lot of ambiguity, but seventeen is not just somewhere between those positions; seventeen is the age of enlistment in the United States armed forces. The lyrics tug her younger without her having to *be* younger. The passion unfolds over a summer, which the narrator remembers from years later, joyously. The song's organizing metaphor evokes a sweetness expanded by the passing of time. Deana figures nature as a producer of fruit, while Garth—who sings about lightning and burning—figures nature as a producer of violence.

Both songs are trying to establish plausible balances of innocence and autonomy but do so in opposite ways. Garth's narrator is an employee, a manual laborer; his physical strength is hedged by economic vulnerability and ambiguous youth. Deana's narrator is the granddaughter of the employer. She is nearly an adult. Her lover is a college student, presumably not so far from seventeen himself. For the sake of maintaining the song's core sweetness, he cannot be any older than that. And her age cannot be so ambiguous. And her grandfather has to remain within the boundaries of the song, within shouting distance. These configurations of agency are also freighted messages about gender, which is why I am so interested that Garth sets his story in such vastness. He needs to limit his character's sense of power in order to evoke a degree of innocence, and he does this by making a mystery of the character's age and making an island of his physical world. Isolation is the prerequisite for their passion. The story must occur in a context in which nothing else exists, because male passion is a form of male joy, and the way to express straight male joy as beautiful is to depower it—uncouple the man from the political and cultural dominance of his masculinity, which otherwise pollutes his joy because a polluted agency is what allows the joy to exist. This uncoupling is a metaphysical project because you have to separate the man from everything that empowers him, things like "adulthood" and "space" and "time." He has to be *almost* totally alone.

My fourth grade music class did not care about any of this.

I did not care about any of this right in the moment.

My care for the Garth song was inarticulate, and I'm not interested in the irony of that—being too innocent to understand a story about a loss of innocence—but I'm very interested in why a class, chattering over words I myself didn't understand, still disappointed me.

What did I think they were rejecting?

The arrangement? The style? The genre? Me?

Or just the energetic expression of male emotion—the temporary suspension of the enforced plainness of midwestern masculinity for the purpose of excitement, passion, love, intimacy?

You can see I am leaning toward the latter.

I imagine Mrs. Hanson sitting at her desk reading the liner notes.

I imagine she asked us to bring in a copy of the lyrics.

I imagine she required this stage of review.

I wonder if she read for the actual meaning, or if she read from our perspective.

Here is what the song is about, and here is what the children probably believe the song is about.

I want to remember what songs the other kids brought.

What did they think was so great.

Probably "Walkin' on the Sun" by Smash Mouth.

Probably something from the *Armageddon* soundtrack.

What I do remember is the room. It was the room where I learned to play the recorder. The room where we had watched a small television as John Glenn rode the space shuttle *Discovery* into outer space, becoming the oldest person to ever go up there. Apparently what happened was that John Glenn asked NASA to send him into earth's orbit, arguing that putting a senior in outer space would be useful for scientific research, and NASA told John, Yeah, that sounds fine, and my class watched this incredible moment when John Glenn did the fourth-most important thing he had ever done and none of us knew why it mattered except generally that it was significant for a human American senator to be fired into an abyss.

. . . .

My favorite song was not really by Garth Brooks, but I was unprepared to reveal my actual favorite to the class. As an eleven-year-old, my actual favorite was Shania Twain's "Man! I Feel Like a Woman!" I liked its enthusiasm. I liked the whole album. I liked how the song titles included so many exclamation points. She was having fun. She was doing what she wanted. Her blues had pep. Her confidence had joy. Her joy had nothing to do with being stomped on by a bull. What I remember is standing at the sink drying dishes for Mom while *Come On Over* blazed out of the cassette player, and as "Love Gets Me Every Time" ended I started to hum the opening bars of "Don't Be Stupid" before the song began, and when the bars imitated what I had hummed, Mom said *Wow*.

I don't remember where I first heard *Come On Over* or who bought me the cassette or if I bought it myself from Pamida. I don't remember a single moment of awakening. I don't remember being in my room or in the family's maroon Dodge Caravan when "Man! I Feel Like a Woman!" jumped out of the radio and first recalibrated my understanding of country music, so let me say first how that album recalibrated a lot of other people and then we'll come back to me.

Come On Over has succeeded in a way that will probably never happen again. For starters, it has outsold every album by the Beatles, Elvis, the Rolling Stones, Elton John, Led Zeppelin, Queen, U2, Prince, Bruce Springsteen, Metallica, and Nirvana. It has outsold Taylor Swift's four most successful albums put together. It has outsold Radiohead's entire discography combined. In the year of its release, Garth Brooks—then so popular he was preparing for Central Park's largest concert ever—released an album called *Sevens* that reached number one in three countries. *Come On Over* reached number one in fifteen countries and outsold Brooks by a number larger than the population of Portugal. *Come On Over* outsold Celine Dion's album from the same year by the population of Sweden even though Dion's record featured "My Heart Will Go On" and had the advantage of being advertised in the then highest grossing movie ever. *Come On Over's* sixteen songs produced *twelve* singles. It has outsold every album by a female recording artist ever and every album made by anyone in the twenty-plus years since its release. And while George Strait remains the overall best-selling artist in country music history, *Come On Over* has more than sextupled the sales of every individual album he has ever made. It topped the American country charts for a record fifty weeks, and it did so while making only one reference to a place in the American South or western plains, a lyric in the penultimate track. The album reached people who have never once dreamed of living in Texas. It reached people who have never heard of Tennessee. The best-selling record in American country music history—a genre obsessed with America itself—was written and recorded by a Canadian.

Place seemed, to me, wonderfully irrelevant.

In *Come On Over*, Shania does not sing about rodeos. She does not sing about blood or gravel. She separates country music from its reactionary insistence on pastoral nostalgia, then separates rock and roll from the cruelty of its male chauvinism, and then rebuilds both genres at the same time. She advocates for an ethic not based in rural iconography. She mocks what men have been told to value about themselves—intellect, money, appearance. In "That Don't Impress Me Much," we learn that only one thing impresses Shania: touch. And she means a lot more than that, but I also think she means exactly that: touch. Contact. The very word *impress* is a metaphor of touch. It is about presence. Shania is *effusive* in her presence, *effusive* in her braiding of strength and tenderness, thrilling in her agency and joy, and all this together seemed to make a belief system, which is what I mean when I say that Garth taught me *latigo* but Shania taught me *prerogative*.

. . . .

Once, Mrs. Hanson instructed us to sing Shania.

We were told to sing Shania because we had failed to sing so much else. The situation was remedial. Last-ditch. End of her rope sort of thing.

Mrs. Hanson had tried to teach us about Count Basie and Duke Elling-ton. She had tried to teach us about swing and jazz. We had tried to sing along with "I Got Rhythm," though I can't remember if it was the version by Gene Kelly or Judy Garland or Louis Armstrong. Either way, we struggled to connect. "I Got Rhythm" sounded *old*, which meant it sounded unalive, or maybe what I am trying to say is that we had confronted the fundamental horror of learning about music. The horror of learning about beats and syncopation and measures and sixteenth notes: This whole time, all this music was just *math?*

So we sang it like math, if you hated math.

Our singing was flat, basically, and what I mean by flatness is that we tried to match our little voices to flat notes on a flat page. Instead of singing with our throat and guts it was like we sang with only our teeth. Like we tried to squeeze the sound out the bones of our mandibles.

What our teacher emphasized about Shania was the dexterity. The looseness. The playfulness. Shania bounced, flared, took on each lyric and made it come alive using her own aliveness; she transmitted her aliveness through the lyric and into the song and out into the world and that's what singing was. Or so begged our teacher, who I now believe had hoped we might see Shania as a kind of *jazz*, and that we might better understand the early twentieth century, might better hear the dexterity of the past, its spark, its bounce, if we came to it via this contemporary person.

Maybe she realized it was a mistake to move forward in time.

Maybe she realized understanding the past would necessarily mean *reverse-engineering* the present, and *reverse-engineer* means, if we're being generous, to analyze, and if we're being less generous it means to destroy something meticulously. She wanted us to develop an appreciation for music, namely the blues, and in particular the way swing had informed rock and roll. We would eventually sing "Respect" along with Aretha Frank-lin. We would sing "(I Can't Get No) Satisfaction" along with the Rolling Stones. We had to get there first. The teacher viewed *Come On Over* as a problem-solving record.

As a last resort, Mrs. Hanson tried to connect with our lives.

She put on the opening tune from *Come On Over.*

The album happened to be lying around.

She printed off the lyrics and passed them around but I didn't need them.

I remember sitting in a blue plastic chair understanding that we were now going to study "Man! I Feel Like a Woman!"

We didn't have sheet music but I tried to focus on what wouldn't have been inside the notes anyway.

Even the opening bars had some buoyancy. Some prerogative.

I tried to make my voice bounce.

I tried to let my voice bounce.

I listened to the way Shania was doing it. She wasn't just imitating flat notes on a flat page. She wasn't just putting her voice into the shape of a music note. The note suggested. Nudged. Her voice followed its direction beyond the direction, so she was lifting off from the note with her whole body. With her aliveness. Like what the older singers had been doing except I hadn't known them already, hadn't heard them coming from the cassette player in the kitchen. Mrs. Hanson wanted us to understand what we already loved so we could see where it came from, and knowing the place it came from would deepen the love downward and expand the love outward and add to our—let me say *my*—add to *my* conception of love that it is owed across time, and that to live in response to what is owed across time is one variation on the word *respect*.

In short, I tried to sing.

· ·

I learned the word *equanimity* from Tolstoy. (This was later.) When I read the word, I looked it up. When I read what it meant, I thought, Oh, like Dad. When I was younger, I admired men who were soft-spoken. Their composure seemed like humility, maybe even reverence—ceding the floor, respecting how other people inhabit space. It seemed like the only alternative to the masculinity of force and arrogance. But I must've gotten something wrong about it. I think I am often presenting myself as a flatness, a plainness, or declining to present myself at all, then acting like this evasion of personality is a form of grace. It used to seem very important to be inscrutable. If I am inscrutable, and someone figures out what I am thinking or feeling, it means I am very humble for making them do so.

What happens early in *Anna Karenina* is that Levin sees Kitty at the ice rink: "He knew she was there by the joy and fear that overwhelmed his heart." Levin—the farmer, who we already understand represents Tolstoy himself—wants to approach Kitty but is trying to play it cool. He envies the other skaters who are nearer to Kitty on the ice: "To Levin they all seemed chosen and lucky because they were there, close to her. It seemed that with perfect equanimity the skaters went ahead, came abreast of her, even talked to her, and enjoyed themselves quite independently of her, taking advantage of the excellent ice and good weather."

Levin compares Kitty to the sun, brightening everything, so bright he can't even look, yet seeing her everywhere because of the ubiquity of her brightness.

He envies those who can look more directly.

How they are so composed even when confronted by the genius of her.

What Levin seems to forget is that probably none of the other skaters are in love with her.

None of their hearts are overwhelmed by joy and fear.

Their *perfect equanimity* is an absence.

Their composure is a deficiency of thrill.

. . . .

I moved to California in 2012 and then Oregon in 2014. For a little nostalgia, I listened to country songs on my long runs. I placed the songs strategically on my playlists so they would occur during my runner's high. I synchronized the songs to my joy: "Heads Carolina, Tails California" and its knockoff "What about Now" by Lonestar. I included from Garth Brooks both "Rodeo" and "Standing outside the Fire"—its fiddle riff sounded to me like the exact feeling of an endorphin rush. I included Garth's "When You Come Back to Me Again," a doubly nostalgic song because it plays over the final scene of the 2000 thriller *Frequency*, a movie my brother and I watched over and over as teenagers. The movie is a double helix of cinematic cliché and cultural nostalgia. Ham radios allow for communication through time. A murder mystery depends on 1960s baseball trivia. Dennis Quaid rides a motorcycle, then a firetruck. In the first act, a ten-year-old Michael Cera holds up the gun that will be used in the climax to defeat the villain. The effects of the gunshot will reverberate through time. Changes in the past will percuss the present. The villain will not just die but vanish.

Frequency ends with the main cast playing baseball in a sandlot beneath some important New York bridge while the piano of "When You Come Back to Me Again" overexplains their emotional condition, which is a renewed belief in the resilience of family. The song always reminds me of this final scene, which is to say it reminds me of something other than the movie's actual conflict, which is the serial murder of women. The song reminds me of what happens after the conflict is solved and the characters are playing baseball and the movie's hero, Jim Caviezel, who would soon become world-famous in his role as Jesus Christ, hits a home run and rounds the bases in slow-motion. The song led through my past to this movie that worships the past, and back, a density of nostalgia that now makes my throat close up a little.

After 2016, I stopped listening to any of it. The whole genre seemed suddenly threatening. The election had revealed nostalgia as an act of demolition. Nostalgia justified cruelty. It inspired domestic terrorism. I felt sick about nostalgia both as a form and as content; both the act of being reminded and the place I was being reminded *of* felt newly dangerous. The music reminded me of place, and the place reminded me of people whom I had thought of as composed but who had concealed something in their composure—composure not just as a determined gentleness but as a withholding—and I know it's not a very serious thing for a privileged person like me to become disenchanted with songs I enjoyed mostly as a matter of retrospect, but I do mean to say that estrangement toward place, which is an estrangement toward self, can take surprising forms. I found joy in a certain music, and shame formed inside that joy and bled its way out.

. . . .

But lately I have been listening to Shania. Shania who isn't quite country. Shania who seems not responsible for the election because she isn't an American citizen. Shania who has a determination for joy, an enthusiasm for joy, that seems uniquely enduring. Or who seems maybe uniquely capable of emerging from a flawed, troubled culture still lit up by a sense of welcome and a sense of love.

Shania who was never about the past, but for one more moment I am going to be.

At age eleven, one of the songs I especially admired from *Come On Over* was that penultimate track, "Rock This Country!," in which Shania gets more overt about her cross-genre work. The song is enthusiastic about hybridity. The chorus of "Rock This Country!" features a call-and-response between the power chords of an electric guitar and the excited racing of a fiddle. Shania sings the word *rock*, followed by the electric guitar, then the word *country*, followed by the fiddle. "Rock This Country!" is emphatic. The song is crazy fun. The song provides examples of which parts of the country are going to get rocked, and these include Texas, sure, but also Minnesota, Nevada, Mississippi, and Utah. The only song from *Come On Over* that name-checks American geography does so to diminish any superiority of one place over another. The point is not *somewhere* but everywhere. Her fun is egalitarian.

For Shania, this was a new approach. *Come On Over* followed her 1995 release *The Woman in Me*, which operated more squarely in the country aesthetic. Its first single, "Whose Bed Have Your Boots Been Under?," entangles two notorious mainstays of country music—men's boots and their infidelity—over a fiddle, steel guitar, and honky-tonk piano. Its second single, "Any Man of Mine," has a mostly traditional country-western production; a backing vocalist imitates the lonesome twang of Dwight Yoakam over a rhythm built for line dancing. *The Woman in Me* is palatable to a narrower crowd. "Any Man of Mine" spent two months atop the country charts and still reached the Billboard Hot 100 but peaked at thirty-one.

The Woman in Me epitomizes what *Come On Over* transcends.

Maybe a better word is *transgress*.

"Rock This Country!" felt transgressive.

Come On Over felt transgressive.

I had always adhered to the eponymous advice in Alan Jackson's song "Don't Rock the Jukebox" from his 1991 record *Don't Rock the Jukebox*. In the song, Jackson asserts that rock and roll is unsuitable for heartbreak. The story is about separating from a romantic partner, which makes Alan feel lonely and sad. The sadness reinforces his affection for country music. He wants to listen to George Jones. He does *not* want to listen to the Rolling Stones. He believes an impenetrable barrier separates country and rock, and he believes the country side makes a stronger claim to the emotional situation of heartache—that the fiddle is the proper rhetoric of human pain.

What I hear Alan saying now is different. I don't think he is worried about genre. If he cared so much about genre, he would understand that "Don't Rock the Jukebox" is country music about not listening to rock music, expressed in the form of a blues tune, which is the exact thing those genres have in common. Alan is not aching in the direction of genre. He is aching in the direction of time. He aches for the past. He aches for the kingdom of familiarity. He seeks echo: play me a song I have already heard in a voice like mine with an instrument like mine describing feelings like mine.

The song you are supposed to play on the jukebox is not by George Jones.

The song you are supposed to play on the jukebox is "Don't Rock the Jukebox."

The genre he advocates for is *self*, especially *past self*, which makes the song less an indictment of rock music than an indictment of the fact that some people are not Alan Jackson.

Some people have never played a song on a jukebox in their entire lives.

If you've never played a song on a jukebox, the thing to understand is you're playing it for the room.

The song isn't just about you.

The song isn't just *for* you.

The song reconfigures everyone's present moment.

A jukebox is about the present.

A jukebox is about the public.

A jukebox is especially about the public dancing.

Jukebox comes from the dance *juke*, which was named for the kind of bar where that dancing took place. The bars were called *jukes*, and they were part tavern, part brothel. People went to the juke for dancing and liquor and sex. They went for pleasure. Joy. The word *juke* comes from a version of Creole, adapted from a term brought to the United States from West Africa by enslaved people, which means the word *jukebox* carries inside it an echo of American chattel slavery, and so to argue that the jukebox should be used to play only country songs, written and performed mostly by white people, or to figure the jukebox as being especially capable of expressing the feeling of any particular white person, maybe requires a certain nerve.

. . . .

A young white man needing to learn about prerogative: I know. I was its fount. Its spring. But what prerogative seemed to mean from Shania's context clues was autonomy plus confidence, and I felt lacking in both. I was too young for real autonomy and too not-at-all confident whatsoever. Shania made prerogative seem like individual agency on turbo. It was an antithesis of stoic, macho composure. It was agency made fun. It was agency made beautiful.

But prerogative is not just personal. It is also public: *the exclusive right and power to command, decide, rule, or judge*. Prerogative implies *governance*; it means a source of authority. It is not just agency but control. I hadn't gathered that from the song. Shania seems to use *prerogative* only in the personal sense. She has the power to judge herself for herself. She has the right to pursue joy, and that joy is synonymous with—or a kind of essence of—womanhood.

The thing about *Come On Over* generally and "Man! I Feel Like a Woman!" in particular is when Shania sings about wanting to be *free* and *wild* and *crazy*, I trust her to be those things. I trust her idea of fun. I trust her movement toward joy. I trust that she is not going to kill someone. She is using a word that means *exclusive right*—a word that empowers someone over a public—and she is using it only in the sense of happiness.

The eleven-year-old me is not getting this message from the fellas.

The men are obliterating their guitars.

They are brooding over romantic failures.

They are choosing to fathom tenderness in moments when technically it is victimization.

They are responding to painful emotions by traipsing off to Wyoming to lash themselves to the backs of livestock.

They are staring out at land so flat it curves away from the eye and they are seeing this huge open place and thinking this is what my love is like, I am this whole place and this whole place is me and together we are freedom but when the men talk about freedom it sounds ominous, like even when they are moving toward joy they are making a lot of digressions and cul-de-sacs into pain and harm and let me give you an example of what I mean by trust.

In 1995, Daryle Singletary's "Too Much Fun" hit number four on the country charts. In the song, he asserts the impossibility of *too much fun*. Singletary believes fun resembles beauty, in that we should allow for its infinite abundance. We should refuse any limitations on fun. Singletary argues his idea with two examples: in the first example he is driving a pickup with a bunch of his friends in the back and he is disgruntled when a police officer pulls them over for driving down the road like that, and the second example of maximum fun—hyper-abundant fun, the sublime horizon of fun—is *getting in a bar fight*.

Here is a story in which men dream of their greatest possible happiness.

In which men consider the furthest vectors of human joy.

In which men concuss each other, get bounced from the bar, and keep drinking elsewhere.

In which the narrator describes his desire for fun as a storm, as a *cyclone*.

What a romp.

So no, I don't trust Daryle with fun. I don't trust him with desire or joy. I'm glad a law enforcement officer pulled him over and I encourage the officer to issue a citation. The man seems dangerous. The man seems drawn to danger. The men often seem drawn not just to the prospect of hurt but to the *unpredictability* of hurt. I am talking about the gender politics of reck- lessness: Shania is singing about the radical importance of welcome—*come on over* as an ethic, an assertion of embrace, an invitation to connectivity, a counterpoint to the valorization of aloneness (come on over!) but a lot of times on the album she is also just singing about dancing. She wants to go dancing and you should come too. She wants the body to emerge into an artform, she wants to rise into a temporary ecstatic wildness, an alive- ness, a personal freedom, and both of these things—the emphatic sense of welcome and the emphatic performance of the artful self—are dangerous, and that danger is gendered, and that means the music, as heard by me, as admired by me, is still a kind of fantasy. Let me put it this way: *Come On Over*'s title track—a feel-good anthem about the joy of gathering—uses an electric accordion that imitates the sound of a xylophone, a sound that is meant, I think, to evoke a kind of "island" music, a white idea about music produced in the Caribbean. The song is about relaxing. It's about welcome. It's upbeat but measured in its jauntiness. It seems designed to be emphati- cally harmless. But then there is this sound that brings to my mind the word *colonial*, and there is Shania, in one live performance of "Come On Over," wearing extensions in her hair, wearing these kinked braids. Hair that is decidedly not for white people but hair that evokes for some white people like me an image of how someone might style themselves on a vacation to an island resort that has been carefully organized to serve their needs and where that service is done by people of color. Or let me put it this way: In "Rodeo," Garth uses the word *joy* and he uses the word *pain* and he uses these words very close together like they are Escher hands drawing each other—the hand of *joy* drawing the hand of *pain* which is drawing the hand of *joy*—and I'm not saying he's wrong but I always flinched at how much he pursued hurt as the sole mechanism for producing joy, and what I hear in Shania is when she produces the hand of joy she is not infatuated with where that hand comes from. She is not even *interested* in where it comes from. The joy has to seem to come from nowhere, drawn by nothing. She is adamantly concerned with *presence* only, and I know I admire that for a reason.

And Grinding Cry of Disaster, or Notes on *Home Improvement*

. . . .

The joke about Wilson was his obscurity. Something always concealed half his face, usually the lower part. The other characters never saw him fully, though sometimes they tried to look. Sometimes Tim stretched his neck, trying to peek over the fence, but he never succeeded. Not because Wilson dodged or avoided his glance. Wilson concealed himself with a degree of ease, almost grace, like his entire personhood organized itself around this one conspicuous, indestructible modesty.

. . . .

I watched *Home Improvement* when new episodes aired in prime time, especially later seasons, during the mid- to late-nineties, but also in syndication, which began in 1995, when I was eight. I watched the reruns every weekday after the news. The show was about a white family, the Taylors, living in suburban Detroit: Tim was the protagonist and patriarch. He had a wife, Jill, and three rambunctious sons. Tim hosted a cable show called *Tool Time*, a show within the show. The main joke about Tim was his destructiveness.

He was always electrocuting people or breaking things or accidentally lighting structures on fire.

Tim had a turbulent streak.

Tim injured the piano teacher.

Tim injured his middle son's girlfriend.

Tim injured his middle son.

Tim injured himself.

The injuries often sprang from his catchphrase: *More power!*

He added a jet engine to his lawn mower.

He upgraded the barbecue, the stereo, the dishwasher, the bedroom.

He wanted speed, volume, horsepower, superlative combustion. He sought risk. He often proclaimed his desire for *more power* in a way that reminded you of the power he already had. A lawn mower is pretty expensive already, not to mention the accessorized jet engine.

But enough about Tim.

Or just a little more about Tim: The formula for an episode required Tim to make a mistake, then go to the backyard for Wilson's counsel. Tim would look to the fence and ask, *You over there, Wilson?* because the fence stood so high he couldn't see. Wilson was always over there. *Heidi-ho neighbor*, he'd say. Wilson was often in the middle of some eccentric activity— whittling a figurine, making homemade yogurt or shoe polish, trying to balance an egg during the vernal equinox—and Tim would interrupt to explain his problem. Wilson listened, placing his arms on the crossbeam of the fence, eyes looking over the slats, lower face concealed.

Wilson's guidance came from philosophy or literature or social science. He quoted from Aristotle, Seneca, *Hamlet*, Corinthians, Immanuel Kant, the English poet Robert Herrick, the English novelist John Boynton Priestley, and the English zoologist Desmond Norris, or if not a direct quotation, Wilson told of an ancient proverb or described the behavioral patterns of Russia's saiga antelope. Wilson knew a tidbit of scholarship that applied to every possible conflict in Tim's life. The advice always confused Tim, so Wilson paraphrased in more familiar terms. Tim strained to understand. You see, Tim wasn't a *book* person. He wasn't a *morality* person. He wasn't even a *kind* person very much of the time. It was supposed to be a credit to his character that he worked so hard to internalize these ideas about how to be a good man, like it showed how deeply he cared for his family that he ventured so far outside his nature. You got the sense that Tim viewed being a good person as sort of pretentious.

I started thinking about *Home Improvement* because Wilson and Tim interacted across a divide that seems improbable to traverse now. They are such different men. They see the world in divergent, often incompatible ways. Tim is arrogant, zealous, competitive, often selfish, sometimes cruel. Wilson is reserved and patient. Esoteric. Impractical. Somehow they trust each other. Tim really listens. He labors to understand Wilson's guidance and then tries to act on it. Wilson respects Tim, never begrudging his more brazen masculinity. I don't want to sentimentalize a fictional friendship, but I'm interested in the way *Home Improvement* put these specific men on the edge of each other's lives. The show created a gap for Tim to cross and created a Tim who would want to cross it. Who would at least try.

The poet and essayist Wayne Koestenbaum writes that "the category 'a kindhearted person' is a construct meant to promote unhappiness, and that no person is uniformly kind from dawn until dusk. Kindness erupts in specific, tiny moments, and then it vanishes." Which means Tim doesn't fail to be *a kindhearted person* so much as he fails, in my opinion, to undergo enough tiny vanishings.

In some ways, the Taylors led an unrecognizable life. My family in eastern Iowa didn't have a dedicated dining area. We didn't have an attached garage with a door that opened into the kitchen. We didn't have an air conditioner, a bread box, a fireplace, nearby professional sports. We didn't have cable to watch the kind of show Tim hosted. And vice versa: The Taylors didn't have a machine shed or a barn. They didn't have cats or dogs or a treadmill. The boys lacked a LEGO city. Tim lacked a golf cart. They had less land. That was really the crux of it: they had less privacy. My parents liked our position in the almost-country, just within the city limits of Washington, Iowa, but down a gravel road. They liked having their own space, how our yard abutted only fields. Our nearest neighbor was Crane Foundry, an industrial plant that manufactured valves and pipe fittings. The factory stood just beyond the north field. My family was not supposed to live on this parcel in the first place—the zoning of our property was industrial—which also meant no one could move in next door. The nearest home was a mile away. The very premise of our lifestyle was that Wilson did not exist.

. . . .

Neighbor implies a family's edge. The person living across the fence is a reminder of where one's belonging stops, where autonomy complicates. On the midwestern plains, crowding feels ridiculous. There is not much to gather around and no grandest vista to compete for. If you are living on the plains, you might as well enjoy the vastness. Call it sovereignty. Call it room to move. It occurs to me how the sitcoms of that time, set in the Midwest, still embraced water: *Family Matters* was set in Chicago, *The Drew Carey Show* in Cleveland, *Home Improvement* in Detroit—all cities that adjoin the Great Lakes. Television never had the guts to landlock characters. TV refused to contemplate our plain-ness.

. . . .

I've lived in western Oregon for six years now. I return to Iowa every year or two. The old neighbors are gone. The Crane factory closed in 2003 when the company transferred production of its valves to China. Across the street from Crane was the Modine factory, which closed two weeks before Christmas 2016, when production of its cooling systems moved to facilities in Mexico and Missouri. The Crane closure left 70 people without jobs. Modine terminated more than 200, including my uncle. These factories were our closest neighbors, though I never set foot in either building. I had to Google what things they made.

. . . .

In 2005, when I was in high school, a new neighbor moved in down the gravel road. A biodiesel refinery now stands on twenty-seven acres, where a field used to be. The refinery produces more than 70,000 gallons of biodiesel per day, made from vegetable oil, soybean oil, canola oil, and animal fat. I am learning this from a two-minute promotional video the company uploaded to YouTube three months ago. The video has nine views. I'm watching in my browser's stealth mode, so the Recommended Videos are likely based on the viewing habits of the other eight people who watched. The recommendations include these:

- "soldiers coming home surprise sister"
- "The Best Golf Tips to Strike Your Irons Solid and Pure"

And Grinding Cry of Disaster

- "The Ultimate Extreme Make-Over: 1 Corinthians 15:35–49"
- "'The most horrific displays of hate I've ever seen': Portland police describe protests"
- a Fox News segment called "When do we get America back?"

. . . .

The joke about Wilson feels different now, in the pandemic, when most people cover the lower part of their face in public to protect against the coronavirus, which has killed more than a million people worldwide, including my grandfather in April. Now we are all wearing masks. Now we are all Wilson. If someone chooses to not be Wilson, I scold them in my head. I curse them. I keep reading how men especially are resistant to wearing masks. Recently, I saw a man in the grocery store not wearing a mask even though the store required them, and a governor's order required them, and basic decency, I felt, required them. But there he was. Him and his whole face. It stilled me to see him—an exposed human mouth in the bread aisle. It was hideous.

. . . .

A few weeks later I saw a man in a different grocery store open-carrying a handgun. The gun was holstered on his belt as he walked through the store. He wore a black neck gaiter extra high on his nose and a cap pulled down low. He was young. Lanky. I hated him immediately. He was accompanied by an older man with gray hair who had decided not to bring a firearm to the grocery store and who wore a face mask in the usual way, and no hat. The older man paid for their twenty-four pack of Rolling Rock, and the two walked to their white sport utility vehicle. I know what they drove because I felt compelled to track them through the store. I watched as they paid, as they exited, as they walked across the parking lot.

Seeing the gun in the grocery store felt a lot like seeing an entire human face in the bread aisle.

My brain clenched onto this singular fact. *Here is a source of harm.*

. . . .

The season 1 finale revolves around the Taylor family stereo: Tim and Jill are in the living room. Tim turns up the volume on the family's sound system. Jill is sitting on the couch trying to read. If you look closely, you can see she is reading *Backlash: The Undeclared War against American Women* by Susan Faludi. The book was first published in October 1991, shortly after *Home Improvement* aired for the first time. By the season 1 finale, *Backlash* has sold more than 200,000 copies. It's a national best seller. On the couch, Jill appears to be working through the book's first chapter. Perhaps she is reading these words: "The truth is that the last decade has seen a powerful counterassault on women's rights, a backlash, an attempt to retract the handful of small and hard-won victories that the feminist movement did manage to win for women. This counterassault is largely insidious: in a kind of pop-culture version of the Big Lie, it stands the truth boldly on its head and proclaims that the very steps that have elevated women's position have actually led to their downfall."

Jill has a hard time focusing because of the noise. She looks up from the book and asks Tim to lower the volume because it's hurting her ears. Tim refuses and in fact *denies it's hurting her.* He cranks up the volume even more. He cranks it so loud the system fails. The speakers are ruined, which gives Tim the idea that he should buy a new, more powerful stereo, a system that can more easily handle the degree of volume Jill had said was painful. Reluctantly, Jill agrees to replace the stereo but asks for something modest: "No boosting, no rewiring, I want something simple I can turn on." She asks him to consider her feelings. You can see where this is going.

Enter Wilson.

Heidi-ho neighbor.

Tim sits in the backyard reading the instruction manual for the massive sound system he just bought. He has already ignored Jill's wishes but explains the dilemma as if it still exists in front of him. Wilson listens. Wilson ruminates on the masculine desire for music's physicality. How music is anatomical. It's felt in the body. Men wish to experience art against our bones. To make his point, Wilson tells Tim about the Greek poetic form of the dithyramb, what Wilson calls "a poem with wild and irregular rhythms," performed in ancient times by dozens of nude men with drums. To demonstrate the power of a dithyramb, Wilson performs some lines from Aeschylus. Wilson doesn't give any context. He doesn't tell us what's happening in the scene. He doesn't explain that the siblings Electra and Orestes stand at the tomb of their father, Agamemnon, planning to avenge his death. Wilson doesn't explain that these lines are spoken by the chorus. He just goes right into it, deepening his voice, bellowing across their small, green, neatly manicured sitcom yards. Here goes Wilson:

My flesh crawls while I listen to them pray.
The day of doom has waited long.

O pain grown into the race
and blood-dripping stroke
and grinding cry of disaster, moaning
and impossible weight to bear.

I don't understand Wilson's point beyond the idea that art is loud sometimes. Often his advice is like that: he gives Tim a historical example that
serves as permission for Tim's bad behavior. *This is the way men are,* he
seems to be saying. *It's simply our nature.* Performing the poem is not
technically a *lesson.* Tim doesn't really grow. Or at least he doesn't *improve*
himself as the show's title implies. Rather, he installs the new stereo, and
in the episode's final scene, he gathers the family to listen. He plays an
opera to appease Jill but again cranks the volume. Jill asks him to turn it
down. The sound becomes piercing. The boys cover their ears, but Tim
can't make it stop—he presses the button but the stereo doesn't respond;
its high pitch starts shattering glass throughout the home: The blender
breaks. A vase bursts. The patio doors explode. Tim ducks. Jill reaches for
the boys to protect them from the shrapnel.

When it's over, Tim is unapologetic. He grunts. It's unclear if he learned
anything. It's unclear if his wife using her body to shield the boys will cause
him any alarm, let alone cause a change in behavior. What I gather from
this moment is that the boys will soon become shrapnel themselves, will
soon produce shrapnel, will soon begin to detonate as they see fit. They
may have already learned that arrogant destruction is an important part of
their manhood. They may have already learned that a patriarch's chief utility
within the family is repairing the damage he himself has caused. That *more*
power need not exist for the purpose of helping anyone. That *more power* is
itself the good, and that they, as men, will never have enough. What they
are learning to be is insatiable. This lesson is not incompatible with ancient
Greek poetry. Wilson didn't prevent them from arriving here.

· ·

The most recent edition of *Backlash* was published earlier in the year I'm
writing, in 2020, with a new introduction from Faludi describing all that has
changed since 1991 and all that has gotten worse. A lot has gotten worse. A
lot has gotten worse since even the book's latest release.

The year has been a disaster.
The year has been a grinding cry.
The year has really piled on.

Some of the disaster could be characterized as consistent with *the undeclared war against American women*, while some of the disaster is a very declared war, while some of the disaster resists characterization at all. The coronavirus still spreads around the country. Infernos have raged through Oregon's forests, burning thousands of homes, destroying entire towns. For two weeks, the sky where I live turned deep orange with soot and ash. Twelve hours after rain started to clear the smoke, Justice Ruth Bader Ginsburg died, plunging the presidential election further into chaos. Five days later, a Kentucky grand jury declined to charge any of the police officers who, serving a no-knock warrant at the wrong address, shot and killed Breonna Taylor in her own home. Meanwhile, in separate incidents, four soldiers disappeared from Fort Hood, Texas, all later found dead, most notably Specialist Vanessa Guillen, who disappeared in April and whose body wasn't discovered until the end of June. Authorities alleged that a male soldier killed Guillen with a hammer and tried to dismember and burn her body prior to burying the remains off-post. An attorney for Guillen's family alleged the man killed Guillen because she planned to register a formal complaint about his sexual harassment.

The year 2020 is also a census year. It's a year to take measure. It's a year to conduct the tedious, important work of learning about who we are.

One evening a few weeks ago, Jessica and I were watching a crime documentary about a serial rapist who had terrorized California in the 1970s and 1980s. The man was an expert at home invasions. He snuck over fences. He broke open sliding glass doors. We sat on the couch and watched the reenactments. We stared into the screen, glued.

The knock on our door felt like a crashing. *The hell?* Who could it be? No one visits anyone now, or no one is supposed to visit anyone. I went to answer. A woman stood a few paces back, wearing a face mask. I lifted a mask from its hook beside the door and put it on. Rachel explained that she was Rachel from the census. She said our neighbors never responded to the mail-in document or answered repeated knocks on their door, so the census needed us to help count them. Rachel wanted to know how many people had lived next door on the last day of April.

. . . .

The guys who lived there had recently moved. We hadn't met the new people. When did the exchange take place? I turned to Jessica. We both went *mmmmmm?* The dudes were youngish and worked construction. A Chevron oil sign hung in their living room. Most nights, they drank beer in the backyard, in a tall pop-up tent like they were tailgating. They had a space heater so they could drink in all seasons. When did the tent come down? Rachel waited with her clipboard. Jessica and I concluded that two white men in their early to mid-twenties had lived in the apartment in April. I also told Rachel that on the day they moved, one of the guys had tried to bestow on me his fireworks collection, which he claimed was very impressive. I offered this detail as consolation. We had struggled to recall basic facts about our neighbors' life, but we knew about their *life*. I explained about the Chevron oil sign in the living room.

. . . .

I am wondering what the situation would have been like if it had been reversed.

If the neighbor guys had watched Jessica and me carry our things to a truck.

If the census worker had knocked on their door because we ignored the mail.

Uh, yeah, two people lived there in April . . .

Kinda old. Like early thirties. White . . .

They wore those kind of nice boring clothes like if you work in an office . . .

She exercised a bunch. Like you could hear her jumping up and down doing burpees or whatever . . .

One time the guy came over and asked us to turn down our stereo. It was like two in the morning, but a weekend, so I don't know what his problem was. But he seemed grouchy about having to come over, like he wanted to say something a lot sooner but he couldn't bring himself to do it, but like dude that's on you.

. . . .

In *Backlash*, Faludi argues that each movement of American anti-feminism emerges from a *crisis of masculinity*. Men observe slow advances in women's equality, panic at the perceived loss of power, and reassign their distress so that equality itself seems to be the source of every problem in a woman's life, regardless of whether that problem empirically exists. Men decide that women are unhappy in their new careers, unhappy being single, depressed by their new, tenuous autonomy. The unhappiness might not be provable in any study, but the cause for these afflictions is still feminism, which must be stopped and its gains reversed. The implication is that masculinity exists only as a power structure; there is little or no male identity beyond authoritarianism. Even the faint promise of equality sends masculinity into crisis because the identity is rooted in power, and power is relational. Power has an object. *More power* requires more subjugation, more shrapnel.

. . . .

A crisis of masculinity sounds less like a sociological event than a scientific way of naming the plural. A murder of crows. A convocation of eagles. A crash of rhinoceroses. A crisis of men. Recently at work, I overheard an older white man tell another older white man it was good seeing him at the hardware store the other day. He called the store *the last bastion of manliness.* He really used those words, and sincerely. The last bastion of manliness is a Home Depot just south of the grocery store. The bastion has a helpful staff, a garden center, and a self-checkout.

. . . .

A bastion is a defensive fortification, the place from which you repel an assault. The upside of crisis is how it allows for this fraternity. Crisis provides a cause. You have brothers in the fight. You have a redoubt. You can work together to repel the attack. You can build up a lot of fences.

. . . .

I'm not sure why I described the store as having those characteristics: helpful staff, garden center, self-checkout. Probably I was trying to subvert the image of Home Depot as a manly domain, but those examples are all congruent with stereotypical American masculinity. The self-checkout encourages faux-self-sufficiency. Plenty of men garden. Maybe the thing about Home Depot that most disrupts *the last bastion of manliness* is the motion-activated doors at the entrance. The un-harassed crossing of a boundary. A technology of welcome.

I don't understand why the producers gave Jill Taylor this specific book to read. What does it mean for her to be reading *Backlash* in May 1992? Did the book's contemporary prominence make it a convenient object? Or is the book a sly political statement? And what statement would it make, given that *Backlash* eviscerates the specific culture that *Home Improvement* reveres? The show's endorsement of patriarchy is emphatic. Jill earns less money than Tim. She does more housework. She plans and cooks the meals. She spends more time caring for the children. A common episode plot hinges on Jill wanting her intimate partner to take her emotions and desires seriously. The show's only prominent female character is essentially an antagonist, and her antagonism is often connected to her wish to be seen as equal. And the Taylors are not a cautionary tale; they are meant to be seen as normal, even aspirational, which leaves me unsure if Jill reading the book counts as empowerment or if it's a mean joke.

If *neighbor* implies a family's edge, the Taylors have only one. Their backyard is the sole exterior space. The audience hardly ever sees the front porch or driveway. The backyard is the only consistent boundary between private and public, and across this one boundary is one man. Not a large family. Not women. Not the Joneses. Not an alternate model for how a big house-hold might organize its domesticity. Just Wilson. I worry his eccentricity is very important, that his strangeness is meant to reinforce the superiority of the Taylor lifestyle. Next door is a man with nothing better to do than balance eggs and memorize ancient Greek poetry. What matters about the performance of Aeschylus is not the story. What matters is that a fishing cap hides the performer's face. What matters is that Wilson seems strange and unknowable and alone—all warning signs, reminding the Taylors to look inward to repair the traditionalist patriarchy that is always almost flying apart. That is why they go to the fence: They know it will turn them back. They know it will confirm the dignity of their own system. They go to the edge because it teaches the center how to hold.

Jessica and I live in a row of condos. Our neighbor on the other side is a white woman in her mid-fifties who lives alone. She's polite and quiet when we pass on the sidewalk. Her backyard has well-tended plants, though I never catch her tending them. When she takes out the recycling, she removes the things that other people have put into the bins in error. Noise never emits from the wall we share, and I wonder if Jessica and I are the loud ones now. If she can hear me playing Shania Twain while I make breakfast, especially when the sliding glass door is open, spilling music into the backyard.

The fence separating our spaces is incomplete, a five-foot-wide panel that doesn't reach the building. The fence is a gesture. There's room to pass around it, and families of deer often stroll from yard to yard.

Why did the show obscure Wilson for so long? According to some pop culture websites, Tim Allen modeled the character on his actual childhood neighbor, who Tim could never see because of his smallness compared to the fence. But what was the point? What does it mean for Tim Taylor the adult character? That's he's childlike? Naive? Solipsistic? Fan theories about Wilson abound. One theory posits that Wilson hides his face because he's in witness protection. Hence why his full name—Wilson W. Wilson—seems fake and evasive. Another theory says Wilson remains out of sight for the same reason a therapist might sit behind their patient during a session, to keep focus on the person attempting growth. Another theory says Wilson secretly fathered one of Jill's children, and as the boys get older Wilson must conceal his resemblance to one of them in particular.

My favorite theory is that Wilson is God. You can't look directly at God. In this version, the carpenter Tim is Jesus Christ, and whenever he goes to the backyard and says, *Are you there, Wilson?* he is looking into the sky, seeking the Lord. When the Lord speaketh, Tim listens. He listens but struggles to understand. Later, when he tries to explain the guidance to Jill or whomever he has wronged, he struggles to articulate the message because he is too earthly, too human. He has a general sense of the wisdom but always carries forth into suburban Michigan a slightly mutilated translation of the divine word.

And Grinding Cry of Disaster

But let's be honest. The theories about Wilson are outlandish. They are conceits to impose meaning where it doesn't exist. Which brings me to the theories about God, which are also somewhat shaky, in places.

My family attended a Methodist church in a large white building across the street from the town's jail and police station. We always sat in the same pew near the back. During the part of the service where we stood to greet the people around us, it was always the same people. The same hands to shake. Same hymns, prayers, covert glances at the clock. I didn't realize until later that the Lord's Prayer has multiple versions. The version we said at the First United Methodist Church included the line about *our trespasses* and forgiving *those who trespass against us*. In the prayer, *trespass* meant sin. Other churches say *debts* and *debtors*, but we lived under the specter of trespass. For us, sin corresponded to an infringement of property. I grew up in a conservative family in a conservative religion in a conservative town—and conservatism cares a lot about property. And now? I'm not a socialist, but I'm more of a socialist than I used to be.

I liked that Wilson was thoughtful and creative. He listened. He wanted to fix things using ideas. And really fix them. Tim tried to resolve a broken stereo and somehow destroyed a vase, the blender, and patio doors. And the stereo was still broken. If the episode continued at that exponential rate, in trying to fix the patio doors he would've burned down the neighborhood, and in trying to resolve that destruction he would've somehow spilled the Great Lakes halfway across the Midwest. Ruined crops in Indiana, Illinois, Iowa, eastern Nebraska. And so forth.

In a retrospective immediately following the series finale, the cast of *Home Improvement* does a curtain call, appearing one by one in the Taylor family living room. Wilson emerges in a cream ministerial robe. Stars and crescent moons decorate the blue lapel. His face is finally revealed. It's beautiful. He pats both cheeks and bows. The core cast follow. The boys. The wife. The husband. They bow. The series ends. Earl Hindman, who played Wilson, dies four years later of lung cancer.

He emerges in the robe because the series concludes with a wedding, between Tim's sidekick from work, Al, and fiancée Trudy. Wilson performs the ceremony, which takes place in the notorious backyard, where a segment of the fence has been removed. The two yards now merge. Rows of chairs are arranged on the grass. Wilson stands between the couple. He holds the Bible awkwardly high so the open book conceals his face. He announces that the power vested in him derives from the State of Michigan and the "church of the celestial moon," which inspires the guests to look heavenward in charmed confusion.

The situation is admittedly confusing. *Celestial moon* is redundant, for starters; the moon is celestial by definition. More importantly, the bride and groom are defying all logic by getting married in Al's boss's backyard, in a ceremony officiated by *Al's boss's neighbor*, a man they hardly know. The ceremony has, effectively, nothing to do with them. Al and Trudy aren't embarking on their married lives so much as they're re-embarking on the married life of Tim and Jill, who first procreated into family and then, more boldly, procreated their concept of family.

I admit my boss has a nice backyard. I once helped him replant the garden and mulch along the garage. (I needed the money and he, apparently, didn't know anyone more capable.) A redwood stands near the fence and looms over the block. Beautiful tree notwithstanding, I'd never want to get married there, if Jessica and I were doing it again. And though I've never met his neighbors, I feel confident I wouldn't want them to officiate. The man who did officiate our wedding was a writer named Ben. His first novel was about a chimpanzee who learns to speak and slowly acclimates into human society. Gets a job. Falls in love. The novel, therefore, includes some bestiality. Upstairs in the hotel, before the ceremony, Jessica's grandmother Mildred turned to Ben. Mildred was a reader. A book person. She said, I hear you are an author. What kind of books do you write?

Ben didn't grow up on a farm in rural western Iowa in the early twentieth century, like Mildred did, so I interpreted him in this moment as crossing a gap. I don't remember what he said. He probably had a canned reply for people he imagined as less than literary. A way of summarizing the story

And Grinding Cry of Disaster

of a talking primate in polite company or among strangers or in moments when you are wearing a suit in a landlocked town's most fashionable hotel.

. . . .

To cross a gap is the only thing possible.

. . . .

We asked him to marry us because he was kind, charismatic, probably the strangest person we knew. Whatever he said about us would be generous and weird. Jessica and I solicited his participation one night at the Mill, in Iowa City, when we were all very drunk, to the point that Ben thought maybe we'd regret our question. He wanted to ensure we were still committed to the idea in the morning, and we were. And I'm glad. I'm glad his eccentricity was cause for invitation. He told us in the ceremony to never settle down, to always keep exploring, which is part of the reason we haven't seen him in years.

The Last Video
Store Essay

. . . .

John and Samuel are two grown men with Bible names pretending to be
assassins in California. Samuel is driving the car and John is riding *shot-
gun,* as they say. John muses about his recent trip to Europe. It's the little
differences, says John. John whose last name is Travolta, like a sports car
named for a lightning strike. Samuel whose last name is Jackson, which is
less distinctive so he fortifies his name with the middle initial *L.* He and
John both wear suits. They look sharp. John explains how the metric system
requires McDonald's restaurants in Europe to have a special name for the
Quarter Pounder with Cheese. Samuel says, So what do they call it?

. . . .

When John says the name. When John practically sings the name. When
John practically disgorges the name like a mama bird. I am listening.

. . . .

I had rented *Pulp Fiction* from my local video store, a franchise called
Family Video. It used to be that you'd go to the video store and wander
the aisles. You'd wander and wander and wander and wander until you
dissolved a little. Until you became the act of wandering, briefly transformed into the unmade decision of how to spend your attention. Odorless

desire clouded the room. How you chose to resist time said a lot about you. Spoke volumes.

. . . .

I am watching in my living room on a television with that faux-wood box design, like the television is pretending to be furniture. I'm sixteen. It's 2004. Southeast Iowa in the new millennium. I'm living in the future. I'm learning how even the most violent men delight in the nuances of culture and language. Samuel echoes the name—*Royale with Cheese!*— and soon after, he and John arrive at their destination, exit the car, fetch their guns from the trunk, enter a nearby apartment, and execute its inhabitant. I had never been to California. Never worn a suit. The man who wrote and directed the movie once worked in a video store himself, and his movies are often *about movies* more than they are about the world around us. Which is to say, renting *Pulp Fiction* means walking into a video store for the express purpose of walking even deeper into a video store.

. . . .

John and Samuel killed people, but they seemed less treacherous because they were *observant*. I wish there was a punctuation mark that signaled, *But I didn't understand any of this at the time.* Say for example the mark could be ø.

. . . .

I live in Oregon now and sometimes people around here make a big deal about the last Blockbuster store, which is in Bend, near the middle of our state. People talk about this Blockbuster like it's the last video store remaining on earth, while Family Video still operates in more than 200 locations, mostly in the Midwest. Family Video had a banner year in 2015. They employed more people than Netflix as recently as 2018. They started selling cannabidiol gummies in 2019. They installed purified water dispensers because some of their customers lacked access to clean drinking water— what you might call *the little differences*. The water dispensers are managed by a subsidiary company whose Instagram account is loaded with stock photos of beaches, waterfalls, tidepools, the dazzling and gigantic sea. The man who runs the water company is third-generation Family Video. He is next in line for the throne. Family Video still earns hundreds of millions in annual revenue.

The Family Video in my hometown closed in 2019. Nine months later, researchers at Northern Illinois University published a logistic regression analysis discussing why some Family Video stores close and others don't. They wanted to know what makes a location vulnerable. What factors decide change. The researchers learned that for Family Video, a smaller population is better. Extremely small towns don't have a Walmart with a movie section and are less likely to have reliable, high-speed internet for streaming movies online. My hometown—population 7,266—has both. The town upgraded its Walmart to a supercenter in 2009. A new traffic light was installed to guide cars into the parking lot.

Streaming is a misnomer. Netflix doesn't stream movies. Movies are available, and you choose one. Your choice initiates the story. That's not how a stream works. A river doesn't begin its motion when you decide to notice the water. To its credit, *streaming* sounds so soothingly natural. You are joining the flow of things. You are aligning yourself with a life force. You are part of the world now. Welcome.

In *Videoland: Movie Culture at the American Video Store*, Daniel Herbert explains it wasn't Netflix that first shocked the video rental industry but the invention of the DVD. Discs were cheaper to distribute and cheaper to own, which meant video stores had to compete with increased movie sales at Walmart and Target. Video stores also had to repurchase their entire inventory in a new format, which was expensive. For the store as well as the environment. Landfills soon heaped with hard plastic and magnetic tape. Herbert notes the irony that one of videotape's largest distributors, Ingram, began as a waste transport business but early on repositioned as a distributor of mass-market consumer products like videos and books. Both business models responded to the tangibility of stories, how a story entered culture as an object with dimensions and weight. A thing that takes up space. But less and less space all the time. Technological advancement happened as a diminishing. The DVD was thinner and critically *lighter*. Required less postage. You could now rent one using the mail.

It's hard for me not to be in awe of this movement toward the irreducible, even when the movement is wasteful and hurts people.

I don't know what it means exactly to no longer need to wander the video store's aisles. Wandering a video store was like scrolling through Netflix with your whole body. But also not quite. You had to pace and pace and weigh your options. The options are all very *here* and so are you. You can't go watch a trailer to inform your decision. You can only examine the boxes. Hold them. The boxes are functionally empty. Each contains a foam block the exact size of a videotape. As a security measure, the tapes are kept behind the counter, and you exchange the box for the tape at check-out. It's hard not to be in awe of a store that depends so much on the dimensions of a videotape but where none of the shelves hold any videotape. You pace and pace and the size of the boxes determines how many steps. You wander and dissolve. The wandering gives shape to desire. The shape is inefficient. It's supposed to be. Wandering is the necessarily wasteful prerequisite to discovery. Wandering performs the self by merging it with the unknown. The unknown transforms into *something* when you bring home the video and watch the story inside, and whatever it transforms into remains part of you regardless of whether it matches the desire that led you there (ø). Sometimes the box lies to you about the story it contains, and the story turns out to be much weirder or grimmer than the box depicted. Sometimes the lie is bothersome. Sometimes it isn't.

Garth Greenwell writes, "One of the great gifts and challenges of desire is that it illuminates who we are in unexpected ways." I agree. I assume *challenges* is a deliberate understatement.

Video store revenue peaked in 1996. DVDs emerged the following year. My family didn't switch right away. I bought my first DVD a few years later as a teenager. I was old enough to drive but not old enough to purchase an R-rated movie. I tried. The cashier at Walmart asked for identification and explained the store's policy. Such a restriction never occurred to me.

At Family Video, the parents on the account set controls about ratings, and our parents let us watch whatever. But now I had to look for something else, and so the first video disc I ever bought was *Behind Enemy Lines*, which I hadn't seen. I hadn't even heard of the lead actor, but it was rated PG-13, which meant it was *for me* (ø).

. . . .

Behind Enemy Lines concludes like this: Owen Wilson, a downed American pilot, is rescued from a shoot-out with Serbian militants on a snowy ice shelf. Three helicopters arrive under the direction of Owen's boss, Gene Hackman. Owen runs toward the cliff's edge while enemy snipers and tanks and henchmen blast apart the snow at his feet. An American soldier descends on a cable from one of the helicopters, and Owen runs to him. Jumps. The hero is midair, reaching toward safety, when a giant statue of the Virgin Mary, which has been standing nearby all this time signaling purity and motherhood and a vague sense of magnitude (ø), explodes. A tank round blasts through her stone heart. Owen reaches the rope. The men embrace. They clutch. Owen is dragged aboard. He rests in the lap of the guy who saved him. The scene's triumphant orchestra music fades to "The Rescue Blues" by Ryan Adams. Its piano returns the story to equilibrium. Owen wipes snot from his nose. The helicopters fly toward sunset.

. . . .

The category PG-13 was invented sixteen years after the rest of the modern ratings system. The industry needed a methodology for showing violent material to a younger audience, so they split the difference between Parental Guidance and Restricted. The new rating allowed for gunfire and death but discouraged blood; gruesomeness was allowed, provided it remained cartoonish and thus hypothetical. *Behind Enemy Lines* depicts the aftermath of the genocide in Bosnia and includes a scene of Owen Wilson hiding from his pursuers in an exposed mass grave, concealing himself in a field of corpses. The corpses are suitable images for teenagers because none of the bodies are bleeding. They are half-buried in mud. Owen is playing dead. The corpses are playing dead. None of it is real. None of it is almost real. Everyone is having a good time.

. . . .

In *Videoland*, Herbert argues that video stores—chain stores, especially—reinforced to consumers the value of timeliness. Video stores had the chance to define quality however they wanted, and they followed the logic of theaters, emphasizing new releases by placing them along the outer wall, while the store's interior was organized by genre, which meant it was organized by emotion. A rack for delight. A rack for fear. A rack for excitement. The perimeter was about newness, and the interior was about feeling. These were the two modes of urgency.

Videotape was first marketed as a method for manipulating time. Per Herbert: one early manufacturer called the video format a "time-shifting" device and encouraged users to record movies from television, especially from HBO, which had recently debuted and, uniquely, omitted commercials. HBO displayed an unbroken stream of story, and video allowed people to preserve parts of the stream. You could step twice into the same river.

As a kid, I didn't have HBO, but my neighbors did. By *neighbors*, I mean friends who lived two and a half miles away, deeper in the country. Later, my brother and I would both drive cars, but our neighbor friends would drive pickup trucks. They had Chevy Silverados. They had four-wheel drive. They lived in the country in a way we didn't (∅), but our interests often intersected. Before they had trucks they had HBO, and they recorded onto a videotape the 1986 feature-length cartoon *Transformers: The Movie*. They gave the tape to my brother for his birthday. I used to think the gift was a little subversive, but it wasn't. Videotape was designed for exactly this. Renting came later. At first, you were supposed to time-shift the television. Our neighbors time-shifted a cartoon about robots. The movie includes a human boy, maybe twelve or thirteen, who hangs out with the good robots to help the target audience place themselves into the story.

You wander and wander and dissolve a little. You are time-shifting. It feels good. Every box on the shelf contains some number of hours. Every box is like a ray of time shooting outward. Every box contains a story, and some of the stories feature characters who are borderline passionate in their capacity for violence. Some of the violent characters are also very observant. They are keen about the little differences. Their keenness hedges their cruelty. It rescues them. It makes them likable. As if they, too, must sometimes dissolve and afterward reform using whatever particles existed in the space in which they came briefly apart.

. . . .

The researchers at Northern Illinois University—Joseph Tokosh and Xuwei Chen—explain that most studies of retail geography over the last sixty years have examined expansion: "An interdisciplinary stream of research emerged on globalizing retail and multinational organizations." But the thing we need to understand now is different. We need to know about decline. About reduction. Diminishing: "The time to build a foundational literature stream investigating store closures has never been more prime." They chose Family Video because its market is obviously receding. It's the only chain left in the industry, and it has closed 200 stores since its peak. How does the process work? How does a thing pull back? What does geography have to do with it? Family Video offers a case study in the present day. We can watch it happen. We can touch a finger to its slow venal hemorrhage. The researchers are careful to note that technically, *one* other chain store still operates. Technically, there is one Blockbuster store in Bend, Oregon.

. . . .

The feature-length cartoon *Transformers* was the last movie Orson Welles ever made. He voiced the villain, an evil planet that devours other planets. By then, the iconic actor's health was deteriorating. He struggled to complete the work. He didn't like the movie (ø). He hated making a movie about toys. Hated playing a toy. Couldn't remember his character's name. Now, his disgust doesn't bother me. The villain seems more villainous this way. More treacherous. Inside the villain is a man who hates everything around him, every character including his own, who resents every difficult, agonizing breath.

. . . .

Like much else in the movie, the treacherous planet transforms into a man. Most things in the movie that transform transform into a man. That is what the movie's tagline means: *More than meets the eye.* Surprise, that sports car is a man. Surprise, that locomotive is a man. Surprise, that tank is a man. That airplane. That fire engine. That planet. Is a man. Is a man. Is a man.

. . . .

The robot story was set in 2005. The opening narration announced *It is the year 2005* . . . which I interpreted as an astonishing leap into the future.

That a year could begin with a different number felt frankly outrageous. Implausible. It was very easy to disbelieve that such a year would ever occur.

. . . .

It's a little distressing, in retrospect, to think how easy it was to disbelieve in the future.

. . . .

The future that *Transformers* imagined wasn't necessarily ambitious. Its world appeared mostly indecipherable from the current world. For the most part, the 1986 version of *Transformers* could've been set in 1986. The alien robot technology wasn't invented later, in 1999 or 2003. In the story, the robot civilization is as ancient as our own. They have been hiding among us for a long time. The crux of this reality is not that a strange new technology skews the future. Instead, the technology already exists. It has always affected human life and history, but we've never noticed it before because apparently humans suffer from a widespread inability to observe our world. Our obliviousness to our environment is categorical. The story is about the failure of perception. The story presupposes an alarming absence of human acuity and suggests what might happen amid such an absence.

. . . .

I imagine Family Video as an underdog. A scrapper. Daniel Herbert wrote an entire book about video rental stores and includes an entire chapter about chain stores but spends all those pages on Hollywood Video and Blockbuster. He doesn't mention Family Video in any meaningful way until the last chapter, until three pages before the end. By then, he's concluding. Describing how the chains are breaking apart, going bankrupt. They are all disappearing. Vanishing. Except one. It hasn't been discussed until now. It didn't matter. Part of the difference is that Blockbuster and Hollywood Video were more common in cities and suburbs and on both coasts. Family Video stayed in the center. Stayed in the smaller markets. Family Video owned its properties while other chains rented their retail space, which meant Family Video expanded slowly, deliberately. It's true, the chain has been through some shit. But it's trying to hang on. Herbert introduces its existence and its survival simultaneously, so both are a surprise, like if Owen Wilson wasn't introduced as a character until he leaps from the cliff. You meet him for the first time midair as he reaches for the rope, for the helicopter, the Virgin Mary explodes in the middle-distance, and you wonder who is this man, where did he come from, thank goodness he is here, thank goodness for whatever place he came from. Owen wipes snot from his nose and you think, what a relatable thing to do.

. . . .

You wander and dissolve. You choose a box and exchange it for the video and bring it home and watch and watch and watch. Sometimes a parent comes home in the middle of your watching and decides to watch however much is left and however much is left includes a scene of heinous brutality and you worry the scene reflects negatively on your taste and personality, as if you wrote the movie and told the actors what to do. You begin to feel responsible for the results of your wandering. But the thing you are responsible for is unpredictable. What unknown are you about to merge with? The events of one story never predict the events of another. John Travolta is here but what does that mean? Is there going to be dancing or no? And here is Uma Thurman. Here is Ving Rhames, whom you remember from the prisoner airplane movie with Nicolas Cage and John Malkovich. You wander and dissolve. John and Samuel kill a man in a shabby apartment. Uma Thurman overdoses on heroin. An unimportant actor rapes Ving Rhames in a basement. Bruce Willis kills a man off-screen. Movies like to pluck up a horror and reform it to align with your wanting. Remove just enough so you can stand it. Scrape the seeds from the jalapeño. Sometimes it gets them all and sometimes it doesn't. You wander and dissolve. You begin to see how many things are *for you* and wonder what it means that this is what you're supposed to want to see.

. . . .

The novelist Naomi Alderman writes, "The power to hurt is a kind of wealth." Both power and wealth are amassed potential. Both are hoarded and thus contrary to the dialectic of lightening and diminishing and becoming irreducible. The banter about European cheeseburgers felt somehow decadent. Luxurious. Maybe it was the suits. Maybe the disposable income for foreign travel. Or maybe John and Samuel's interest for the details enriched them in a different way, or made visible their richness. They have the power to hurt but also the power not to. Which is the same. That was Alderman's point. The power not to hurt always implies the power to have done so. Every tranquility or delight happens in the absence of *something*. It's a mercy they're not hurting anyone right now. And the mercy implies choice. Capacity. Wealth. The first thing wealth can never do totally is conceal itself.

The Last Video Store Essay

My wife and I leave Iowa for California. I have money from the army, which allows us to move into an apartment on the west side of San Francisco, eight blocks up the hill from Ocean Beach. I like seeing the water each morning on my way to the bus stop. I like the neighborhood. The local video store is a mom-and-pop place that doubles as a post office. The city doesn't have many big franchise stores because ordinances limit where chains can do business. Each neighborhood has its own restrictions. Chinatown, North Beach, and Hayes-Gough prohibit chain stores entirely. The city planning code declares, "The standardized architecture, color schemes, decor and signage of many Formula Retail businesses can detract from the distinctive character and aesthetics of certain [neighborhoods]." The city wants to avoid a *homogenizing effect*. They want to promote little differences. I understand this at the time. I savor it. I believe the ordinance reflects warmly on me as a moral person and consumer.

It's true the local video-store-slash-post-office carries a lot of the same movies as Family Video. Just not as many. The store is smaller. It's harder to get lost. Harder to feel lost. The lights aren't as harsh. I can wander and wander and still feel like myself, which probably just means my sense of wandering has expanded beyond the aisles. Become routine. The wandering and selecting from an array of unknown paths and fearing how my choice will define me regardless of its alignment with my beliefs is how a lot of my life works now. The choice itself is only part of the story. Not just the object you take from the shelf but the time you spend deciding to take it. Putting your hand on the box is the midpoint. The fulcrum. You first had to become the person who would put a hand on *that* box.

Movie stores appearing in movies is usually an ominous sign. In *The Lost World: Jurassic Park*, a dinosaur rampages through the streets of contemporary San Diego. The animal destructs the place indiscriminately. The dinosaur chomps down on a traffic light. The dinosaur slams into a city bus, which careens off course and smashes through the front of a Blockbuster, destroying a promotional cutout of Arnold Schwarzenegger. The video store patrons run. Scream. The reengineered predator chases them.

In *Yes Man,* Jim Carrey wanders the aisles of a Blockbuster in Los Angeles. His movie habit implies ennui, if not depression. The trouble with Jim is that he doesn't say *yes* to new experiences. While Jim roams the video store his friend calls to offer a fun night out, but Jim lies about being busy. He keeps browsing. He chooses *300* from the shelf. He chooses the Shia LaBeouf version of *Transformers.* The choices represent absurdist counterpoints to Jim's actual life. He is not one of the strong, exciting people. He is stuck in a routine. For a movie to dramatize existential sadness in this specific way *to a movie audience* is pretty insulting. It's also relatable.

In *Captain Marvel,* when the eponymous extraterrestrial hero falls to earth, she crashes through the roof of a Blockbuster. It's Los Angeles again. 1995. It's nighttime. She wakes in the store's darkened aisles. The ceiling's damaged guts dangle above her. She stands, gets spooked, and fires her weapon at a promotional cutout of Arnold Schwarzenegger. Blasts off his head. Shatters the glass storefront. She mistook him for a threat. Mistook him for the kind of person who would be in the movie she's in. She tries to call home on her communication device but no one responds, so she wanders the aisles. She picks up *The Right Stuff* and examines the box. She chooses the movie about pilots because she recognizes its concept of heroism, one of bravery and speed. What's different is that *The Right Stuff* is about test pilots for the space program. It's a story about exploration. A story more peaceable than her own. She replaces the box on the shelf, steps through the window she broke earlier, wipes the dust from her shoulders, and stands under the blue Blockbuster awning. She pauses to gaze across the parking lot. The area is a strip mall, a common setting for video stores in 1995. Standardized architecture frames the strangeness of her superheroic presence. The moment seems to loom. She seems ready for this place. Her stance has an effortless tenacity. Maybe *ominous* was the wrong word. The potential for violence is *iridescent.*

This essay, like much of its topic, is now obsolete. In January 2021, two weeks after I achieved the confident feeling that I was done writing about Family Video, the company's CEO announced the permanent closure of all their remaining stores. The slow hemorrhage is over. The end came fast.

The pandemic struck like an asteroid, the extinction kind where the impact causes tsunamis that cause shock waves that cause earthquakes and wildfires and volcanic eruptions that broil the atmosphere and smother every living creature with poisonous gas. The pandemic hit like a very big rock from outer space. Hundreds of Family Video employees lost their jobs all at once—that is really the only fact that matters. And yet. I can't help but think the ending is unfair. There was supposed to be more to watch and study, more to learn about the geography of obsolescence. More to learn about how to endure and thrive amid change. I want to reiterate that Family Video didn't just edge out Blockbuster. They didn't just hang on a little longer. They successfully operated inside a culture that already viewed franchise video stores as time markers for a bygone era. You could walk into a Family Video, rent *Captain Marvel*, take it home, watch the hero crash through the ceiling of a Blockbuster, and know the presence of a video store signified a step into a different time. You are now in a moment when *The Right Stuff* is only twelve years old. It's no longer a new release but not yet a classic. The hero plucks it from a rack in one of the middle aisles, the aisles organized by emotion. She is walking through the excitement part of the room. The room looks a lot like other franchises. The room is designed to advance the cause of mass consumer culture, but the special thing is that while the aisles of a Family Video looked mostly the same, they represented, for a while, the possibility for variation within that mass consumer culture. Chain after chain went bankrupt, but Family Video still had customers. Even mass culture could respond to the little differences of a place or region. By unfair, I mean that during the pandemic the entertainment industry stopped making movies for a year, so by 2021 Family Video stores had nothing to sell. By unfair, I mean the erasure of chain video stores will soon appear uniform. It will seem that streaming was invented, so the video stores all vanished. But it wasn't like that. The vanishing had nuance. Some chose to resist it. The way you resisted it said a lot about you. Spoke volumes.

Chelydra Serpentina

. . . .

I don't remember why the fourth grade science teacher, Mrs. Winters, kept a snapping turtle in a bathtub at the back of the classroom, though I can imagine her thinking that animals are part of nature and nature is part of science, but you could rationalize anything that way, like maybe the English teacher, Mr. Kerr, should've kept a snapping turtle in a bathtub because *bathtub* is a noun and *menacing reptile* is a noun phrase. But he didn't. Instead, Mr. Kerr had an old brown barber chair at the back of the classroom, and sitting up high in the barber chair during quiet reading time was considered a prestigious reward. Mr. Sperling, the social studies teacher, had a Sheryl Crow poster on the wall and a little toy basketball hoop and we earned chances to stand behind a line on the carpet and shoot free throws and if we made the free throws he gave us extra credit. Mr. Sperling taught us the meaning of communism and how Kansas was the breadbasket of the world and how Sheryl Crow was brilliant and also very gorgeous. Mrs. Winters taught us how to make a circuit using a battery and wire. Mr. Kerr taught us the helping verbs. He did so by organizing a tournament in which pairs of students stood at the front of the room and competed to see who could recite all the helping verbs the fastest: *Be, am, is, are, was, were, been, have, has, had, do, does, did, can, could, shall, should, may, might, must,* and *being.* The girl I competed against has since died, and Mr. Sperling has since died, and Mr. Kerr's son was the director of the nursing home where my grandfather died, and I still don't know why there was a snapping turtle in the bathtub.

Mrs. Winters had a collection of Boxcar Children books and I checked them out one by one, stories about homeless children who lived in an abandoned train car and solved mysteries; the littlest child had a favorite cup with a crack in the porcelain. I read the books in a day or two, then returned to the shelf at the back of the room to choose the next in the series. Mrs. Winters's choice to domesticate a reptile had cascading effects, and one effect was that the room now carried a distinctive fragrance, a heavy swamp odor, so no matter what was going on it was hard not to notice *something* was making that smell and the something, the joke went, *will rip your hand off* if you get too close. The smell connoted a threat, basically, and I'm not saying I feared the turtle but my awareness was more activated than usual, I had a poise, an alertness, I knew the bathtub had a radius of danger, a hand-bite zone, and the hand-bite zone had a secondary zone beyond that, a zone of lesser risk but still with some risk, where if I wandered off-path I could find myself within the turtle's territory. But even outside its territory, beyond the radius of danger and beyond the intermediate region, was the swamp odor, which reminded me, always, that lurking nearby was an imprisoned dinosaur. The turtle ruled by its smell. The smell was a power move: *I am here, I am here, I am here, I am here.* The turtle emitted an entire ecosystem of sensations, so powerful that the vessel of cleansing it lived within now had a reverse meaning; the bathtub now meant pond scum and the prospect of severed child fingers and this reversal was caused by just one quiet, heavy animal, almost a plant it was so silent and still, which makes me wonder if Mrs. Winters isolated this creature from its proper environment just to prove the unstoppable radiance of nature.

For some reason, Mrs. Winters couldn't just tell us how circuits worked. She gave each student a battery, bulb, and length of wire and disbursed us throughout the swamp room. We each experimented with the objects until we discovered how to illuminate the bulb, then we had to request permission to crawl under her desk into the cubby where her legs usually went and reassemble the invention so only she could see. Mrs. Winters then assigned us a more complex objective, using more wires, more bulbs, and switches, and we had to tinker until we figured out the new arrangement, before again requesting permission to crawl under her desk to demonstrate.

The first arrangement was the most difficult. It required arriving at the concept of a circuit on one's own. Here is what I did: I went to my corner of the room with my battery, bulb, and wire and touched one end of the wire to the battery and the other end to the bulb. I expected brilliance. But nothing. So I reversed the wire, like maybe *this* end had to touch the battery and *that* end had to touch the bulb, but still nothing. I tried again and again. I looked around. I wanted to cheat but we all had our secret areas of the classroom and then the worst possible thing happened: Derek rose and headed for the desk.

The reasons I hated Derek were manifold, but the most recent reason I hated Derek was because during the unit about outer space he gave his presentation about Roman mythology; Derek was super into the Roman gods, and he exploited the fact that some of the planets are *named* for Roman gods as an excuse to talk about them, and Mrs. Winters put up with this bullshit even though his presentation taught us nothing about outer space, unlike my presentation, about *Apollo 13*, which taught us about perseverance and how outer space is a landscape for exploring our most perilous desires, and I admit the movie *Apollo 13* influenced my presentation but only because the movie so expertly depicted how the failed mission in a way succeeded because the men had demonstrated such courage, such heroic wit, what they did was fly into the cruel maw of stars to help with an elaborate science project hardly anyone understood but which mattered less than the journey itself so when the journey erupted into crisis, when the journey revealed itself as man-versus-nature, when the journey revealed itself as man-versus-cold-infinite-drift, as man-versus-sucking-violence-of-heaven, what the men did was use ingenuity and teamwork to blaspheme the void, blaspheme nature by surviving it, what the men did was fly back out of death, a story I more or less explained to the class using a model of the spaceship I made from pop cans and white construction paper and LEGOs while all Derek did was teach us a myth. Still, it was Derek who rose first and headed for the desk, who crawled into the leg nook of the desk, and who, moments later, made a glow emit against the laminate floor, a glow that made me feel now just ruthless with ambition, so I looked back at my bulb, battery, and wire and fiddled and stared and somehow eventually it occurred to me the wire couldn't just go from thing to thing. You had to cause an indirectness. It wasn't about the bulb at all but the wire, the wire was everything, and it had to curve.

Then the bell rang and we rose from our desks and walked to Mr. Sperling's room where he taught us a made-up story about the Trans-Alaska Pipeline. Mr. Sperling often taught using made-up stories. He invented two characters, Fred and Earl, and sent them on misadventures through history, their rambunctious affairs laying the way for modern human existence. In this case, Fred and Earl wanted to build a spit-wad shooter, and they wanted the device to be a marvel. They wanted to blast a spit wad to the farthest reaches of the earth, so they built larger and larger versions of their device until eventually they had made a shooter 800 miles long, a tube that worked so beautifully they realized it could have alternate functions, and eventually the pipe was repurposed to transport oil from the wilderness into civilization where it was refined and then burned in the engines of the buses that brought us to school. Fred and Earl were a memory trick. Mr. Sperling knew we'd remember the Alaska pipeline if we heard it as a story, but the story had to be funny and ostensibly harmless—the story had to be charming—so Mr. Sperling invented these characters and did a sound effect when Fred launched a spit wad at Earl, who stood at the other side of the pipeline: *splat* the spit wad against Earl's face. Mr. Sperling slapped his own cheek to make the noise, then laughed with us.

Indefatigable Zeal

Iowa mesmerized him. This wasn't unusual. It happened in a different time. In 1857, people would rearrange their entire lives to pursue the difficult dream of Iowa. The dream called to people like Franklin Tarbell, who lived with his family in western Pennsylvania. For them, Iowa meant the West. Iowa meant the new, the open, the possible. The Sac and Fox tribes had ceded the land under threat of military force twenty-seven years earlier. The federal government paid the tribes three cents per acre for some of the most fertile ground on earth, which is another way of saying the federal government took the land so they could give it away to someone like Franklin. So his family could make a claim, build a farm, establish a series of routines that would find them oscillating between fear and joy and exhaustion and love. It must've seemed to Franklin like the best possible version of their life existed in Iowa, so he went there, alone, an advance party looking for the site of their future home. His wife Esther was pregnant, but Franklin felt confident that as soon as he found a parcel, she, too, could make the trip and give birth here. Their future daughter, Ida, would describe Franklin's energy for Iowa like this: "His letters tell of the splendid dome of sky which covered it, of the far view over the prairie, of marvelous flowers and birds, of the daily passing along the horizon of a stream of covered wagons, settlers bound for California, Pikes Peak, Kansas, Nebraska; and some of them, he found, were earlier Iowa settlers, leaving the very state which for the moment seemed to him the gate to Paradise."

The plan was risky, and it wasn't his fault when it failed. He had found land. He had found their spot at the gate to paradise, but the damn banks. The young nation's banks underwent a sudden crisis, an implosion of credit, and money for a new farm was no longer possible. Money for anything was no longer possible. Franklin couldn't build a home. He couldn't send letters. He was stranded.

Back in Pennsylvania, Esther didn't know what was going on. She didn't hear from her husband for more than a year. She gave birth to Ida. Perhaps most importantly, she gave birth in Pennsylvania.

Meanwhile Franklin was walking home. It took him eighteen months. He worked brief teaching jobs to pay for each leg in the journey. He walked, then taught, then walked, each step unwinding his dream. But Franklin's botched plan for Iowa cleared the way for different ambitions. As soon as he reunited with Esther and his new daughter, he heard a powerful rumor, and this rumor, too, had everything to do with land. Had everything to do with the fecundity of American ground. In 1860, in response to this rumor's unshakable gravity, Franklin moved his family from Erie County across the state to a place called Cherry Run, a tributary of a creek of the Allegheny River. The child, Ida, was not even three years old. But she will remember Cherry Run. Or more to the point, she will understand it. She will understand the place tenaciously. She will write its story not only in a way that reshapes the place itself but, further, in a way that changes the course of the country at large. But first, she is not even three years old, living in a shanty house seventeen miles from Titusville, Pennsylvania, where the first commercial oil well in America has just been struck.

. . . .

Whom the land belongs to, and what ethical considerations follow from that belonging, is how the story starts and where it goes.

Ida Tarbell grows up curious about nature. She collects bugs and rocks and plants, bottles them, and places her "collections" all over the family's modest home. She gathers leaves and presses them between the pages of her family's books. She thrills in classifying the leaves by shape and color and vein and stalk. She likes the methodology of science. You are puzzled by something and the puzzlement leaps into a question, which formalizes into an experiment, then another, then another, meandering toward knowledge. For instance, one day Ida stares to the bottom of a pond and wonders why some things float but not all things, so she pushes her brother into the water to see what happens. By the time she's thirteen she dreams of being a scientist. By then, her family has moved deeper into oil country. Her father earns money designing and building wooden oil tanks, and when the boomtown around their home dries up he buys a nearby hotel for $600—about 1 percent of its value—dismantles the building, loads the pieces onto wagons, drives the wagons to Titusville, and builds a new home from the parts. In this home made from something else undone, Ida continues her study of rocks and leaves, a study that soon shakes her belief in God. She wants to know: What is the truth of the earth? Where do the rocks come from? How does it all exist? How much is science and how much is holy? In her autobiography, Ida frequently places horror and amazement side by side. Discovery recurs as a sort of intellectual violence. What she learns always has to brawl with what she knows, what she learned before. When Ida attends a lecture series at her church that attempts to reconcile geology and religion, she comes away "fascinated, horror-stricken, confused." She lets the confusion inspire her. She saves her money and buys a microscope.

The story she will eventually tell is happening in the background while Ida becomes the person capable of telling it. In 1870, while her father is moving the family to Titusville, John D. Rockefeller is in Cleveland founding the Standard Oil Company. By the end of 1872, the company controls more than 20 percent of the oil refinement in the United States. Soon after, 80 percent. Soon after, 90. Franklin Tarbell explains the situation to Ida as the situation refigures their lives. He explains that Rockefeller isn't playing fair. That he has made secret deals with the railroads, which are supposed to belong to everyone. Franklin explains that public transportation cuts across everyone's land; the right-of-way is granted to the railroads under the premise of community, the premise that everyone gets equal access. But Rockefeller has stolen the railroads for himself. He is getting special rates, then leveraging those rates to drive out competitors. He has already squeezed out most of the refineries in Cleveland. Rockefeller doesn't respect the ethics of ambition, which is to say the limits of ambition. There is a point where you have to stop, a point where ambition tips into ruthlessness, and Rockefeller has blown past that point. He wants to control every part of the industry in every place it exists.

In 1876, Rockefeller is busy reshaping his monopoly as oil transportation shifts from railroads to pipelines. Land must be gathered all over again so oil can be piped from Pennsylvania to the East Coast, where it can then be shipped to Europe. Meanwhile, Ida Tarbell begins her first semester at Allegheny College. She is one of only five women studying there and the only woman in her class of forty-one. She likes that science can be a method for seeing through time. She wants to locate what she calls the "beginning of life," wants to look inside the smallest atom, where she hopes to see God, or some version of the Almighty, some clue about where and how the spiritual and material intersect. Tarbell delights in being around people who are as curious as she. She writes of a professor who has become fascinated with the work of Alexander Graham Bell: "What I remember best is not the telephone but Professor Tingley's amazing enthusiasm for the telephone. This revelation of enthusiasm, its power to warm and illuminate was one of the finest and most lasting of my college experiences. . . . He did his best to stir you to share his joy." Tarbell rejects the Puritan commitment to labor as a drudge. She wants purpose in her work and she wants joy and excitement and excitability and she wants the excitability as a constant. A phrase she will later use to describe Standard Oil also applies, in a way, to her: she wants *indefatigable zeal.*

It's probably no coincidence that she frames this rapturous quality as *the power to warm and illuminate.* To warm and illuminate, at once, is the power at the center of her story. It's the power of the kerosene lamp, the era's primary means for lighting a home. The kerosene lamp is the reason men began devouring Pennsylvania. They wanted to refine oil into kerosene. They drilled oil for light. They haggled and fought for light. They pumped up so much oil that sometimes it couldn't be moved or stored and the oil drained back into the ground unused. All for light. And it's hard for me to keep this obvious fact in mind, that Standard Oil achieved its monopoly before the Model T was ever conceived. And though some companies refined oil into a lubricant, the big business, and where Standard did all its work, was illumination. The desire was not to move but to see. It had nothing to do with cars, nothing to do with the loud, fast violence of the combustion engine. By comparison, the kerosene lamp was a hearth. In her book *Brilliant: The Evolution of Artificial Light,* Jane Brox reminds us that the kerosene lamp was the final version of *cultivated* light, when people crafted domestic brightness themselves. Kerosene lamps were the most powerful and efficient candle in history, and they persisted longer than they should have, after the technology of gaslights had been developed and made ready for consumers. People hesitated to switch. They wanted to manage the flame. It seemed wrong not to. It seemed contradictory to human nature. Brox compares the kerosene lamp to the candle that allowed early humans to make their first art deep inside caves: "That flickering was a link to the light at the beginning of human time: the kerosene lamp was the apotheosis of the tallow cupped in limestone at Lascaux, the last self-tended flame."

It is the kerosene lamp that required the pillaging of Pennsylvania, so how can we not see that lamp in Tarbell's description of the joy of learning? *The power to warm and illuminate.* The two concepts are inseparable. Light was not just a metaphor for understanding but its mechanics. You needed the lamp to live after dark. It was still, then, a privilege to see with so much clarity. It was still a spectacle. And it's difficult for my modern self to keep this spectacle in its proper context, but I'm trying to hold in mind the idea that Americans first took to burning because of the obvious fact that it was luminous.

. . . .

Fortunately, Ida Tarbell comes around to the notion that human beings are as interesting as rocks and leaves. The shift takes time. First, she graduates from Allegheny College and teaches for two years at a seminary in Ohio, seventy-five miles from Cleveland. She wants to become financially independent, and she sees teaching as the path—combined with a firm belief to never marry, which would limit her freedom to explore and enjoy and confront the world—but her income from teaching doesn't support her in the way she hoped it would. Further, she resents the school's stiff traditionalism, the rote-ness, how students are made to memorize the same questions and answers because these are the questions and answers the teachers have memorized, a genealogy of useless facts passed down across time. She resigns in June 1882 and moves home to Pennsylvania.

Soon after, the Methodist culture of her family yields an opportunity. A pastor is staying at their home. He has retired from preaching and now helps run a colony, a community, for practitioners of the Methodist faith. The community has a reading circle. The reading circle has a magazine. The magazine needs help. So the pastor gives Tarbell a job. She works at the paper for eight years. Her work is still educational. The magazine's readership extends beyond the immediate Methodist community and reaches far into rural Pennsylvania. The magazine includes annotations, footnotes, guidance for uneducated readers on how to approach the circle's texts. Then the magazine expands, and Tarbell writes her first serious article, about suffrage and creativity. Tarbell watches the debates around suffrage with skepticism. The men are saying women shouldn't vote because they don't understand the issues, and the women are saying they don't understand the issues because they haven't been included in anything. Tarbell thinks they're all wrong. Women *are* included. Women do understand. Women are already contributing to the country's prosperity. Women are already thoughtful and creative and engaged. She hears an oft-repeated detail that women have contributed only 300 patents to the entire patent office in Washington, D.C., so she interviews the director and scours the archives. She discovers more than 2,000 patents submitted by women. She writes this story. It is the first.

But again her job interferes with the path Tarbell envisions for herself. She is maybe too cozy, too settled. She wants to keep writing about women. For Tarbell, suffrage is a kind of recurrent intellectual snag. She understands that men are often terrible at making decisions, but why should women be any different, but maybe they are different, maybe women have a unique political efficacy, but how would she know? She wants to keep exploring her gender's revolutionary capability. She begins with the revolutionary women of France. She is intrigued by Madame Roland, a writer and intellectual guillotined during the Terror, and decides to study her in detail, maybe write a biography. To do so, she has to go closer to the place where it all happened. Tarbell decides to move to Paris. Her friends are alarmed. Her boss is alarmed. Tarbell doesn't care. She decides maybe she was never meant to be a scientist. Maybe she was meant to be a journalist, a writer. She decides to start over. She tries something new. She moves to Paris with three girlfriends and $150. She is thirty-three years old.

In Paris, she quickly begins selling articles to American newspapers, mostly in the Midwest—Chicago and Cincinnati—articles mostly about French women. Then she interests *McClure's Magazine*, to which she sells articles mostly about scientists. She earns enough to support herself and continues her research on Madame Roland before returning, in 1894, to the United States with part of a manuscript. The editors at *McClure's* ask her to set it aside to write the biographical treatment of someone else, so Ida writes her first serialized story for *McClure's* about Napoleon, who is irrelevant to the story of oil except that he provides Tarbell a point of reference, a framework, so when she writes the story that will make her famous, she has a sense of scale. She will compare her later subject to Napoleon over and over: "He saw strategic points like a Napoleon, and he swooped on them with the suddenness of a Napoleon." Napoleon becomes a heuristic for deftness and audacity. He becomes the measuring stick for John D. Rockefeller, founder of the business that corrupted Franklin Tarbell's industry. John D. Rockefeller, who would later earn nicknames like the Monster, the Great Anaconda, the Octopus, the Dragon. But Tarbell knows the appropriate comparison is not to animals or creatures. The way Rockefeller devours an industry is not mythic or creaturely but human—it is something only men do. So she treats Rockefeller like a general, and not just any general. Not just any war. He is Napoleon, making war on a scale no one has ever seen.

. . . .

The tanks have been torn out by construction workers. It happened earlier this year, in 2021. The workers arrived at the gas station my parents own, the station my grandparents owned before that, the station that has been in my family since it was a Standard Oil station in the 1960s, then an Amoco station in the '80s and '90s, then a BP station in the early 2000s. Workers dug out the tanks that once held the gasoline because my parents are trying to sell the station, and to attract a buyer they have to transform the property to suit other businesses. Mom is thinking maybe a KFC or Dunkin' Donuts. We are talking on the phone and she mentions Dunkin' Donuts about eleven times. At first, she was more interested in KFC: she got on the KFC website to see about the franchising options, because maybe the person who ought to buy the property doesn't understand how easy it is to open a KFC, and because my hometown used to have a KFC and our family used to go there for lunch after church every week and now the KFC is gone but everyone in town wants it back, so why not on this corner? Mom is doing all this homework so she can try to persuade someone to convert the gas station into a fried chicken restaurant, but actually it costs more than you would think to open a KFC franchise. She says the website says you're supposed to have $1.5 million in cash assets to open a restaurant, so the KFC idea is kinda fading a little.

The problem is nobody wants the property as a gas station. Or rather, one family wanted the property as a gas station, but they couldn't get a loan from the bank because buying a gas station, going into the gas business, is a high-risk venture. It's a high-risk loan. The buyers thought they were a shoo-in for the loan because they had operated gas stations before, but it didn't matter. The damn bank. Turned them down, so the gas station has to stop being a gas station. A crew dug up the tanks. The pumps are gone too. I can't even imagine how it looks. Mom is past all that. She's past the sentimental stuff. She's thinking maybe a Dunkin' Donuts could go there because the town doesn't really have any coffee shops or donut shops, and the location is great, at the intersection of two highways like that.

I've lived on the West Coast for nine years. When I first moved to California and Mom called from Iowa, one of the first things I told her was how the gas station brands are different. California has Shell but not Casey's. Chevron but not BP. She was appalled. Or let me say, she was enthusiastically concerned. My family takes pride in quality gasoline, and lucky for us, the only quality gasoline was the kind we happened to sell, which most recently was BP. But now I had lost access to that brand, which meant my car would be ruined. The engine would melt. Mom asked what happened. *Why is there no BP?!* I said I didn't know. Things are just different here.

But now I know: the reason gas station brands are different here is because Ida Tarbell published *The History of the Standard Oil Company* in 1904, and the outrageous narrative contained therein prompted a congressional investigation of Standard's monopoly of the oil industry, an investigation that resulted in Congress ordering the company's dissolution. Tarbell broke up an empire. Standard appealed to the Supreme Court but lost, and in 1911 the company was forced apart. The dissolution happened geographically: the monopoly was split into thirty-four pieces, including Standard Oil of New Jersey, Standard Oil of New York, Standard Oil of California, and Standard Oil of Indiana—companies that later rebranded as Exxon, Mobil, Chevron, BP, and Amoco. I buy gas at what was once Standard Oil of California while my parents buy gas at what was once Standard Oil of Ohio, which is another way of saying that Standard was the giant that bled giants. Like if you broke apart a world war into many smaller, discrete wars. The industry changed and my family life is different from what it might've been because Ida Tarbell wrote a book.

On our most recent call, Mom talks about slowing down. She doesn't say *retirement* or *vacation*, but she wants to work less. Her tone is casual, but the notion is incendiary. Mom and Dad haven't taken a vacation in twenty years. They always say they're too busy. They've been running the gas station. They've been keeping things going. They have a towing business on the side where Dad pulls vehicles from ditches and shoulders. They have the gas station to keep cars on the road and the tow trucks to respond to the road's dangers and hazards, the ice and snow and white-tailed deer and drivers distracted by text messages or impaired by grain alcohol. Mom and Dad don't vacation. They don't travel or hike or sit on beaches or sip margaritas or visit museums or go on cruises or scuba dive or zip-line or try new dishes at new restaurants in new cities. But now Mom is saying she doesn't want to just work and die, and if things keep going the way they're going that's what will happen. She will have worked and died.

Tarbell first publishes her story about Standard Oil as a serial in *McClure's*. The form allows for momentum. People read a little each month. Many start contacting Tarbell with information. New sources emerge. The story snowballs with greater and greater force. The story is massive and wildly complicated, but Tarbell manages the parts expertly. She understands how it happened and knows where to fit the pieces. She writes the story like she was born to write it, which maybe just means she writes the story like she was born in a specific place; she arrived somewhere and lived there and witnessed it and decides to add to that place the obvious fact of her own unique will.

After the dissolution, Standard Oil remains a prominent brand throughout the Midwest. A crown logo represents one of the new independent companies, Standard Oil of Indiana, which is known simply as Standard Oil. The crown's visibility expands as gas stations popularize during the 1920s, when the number of stations in America increases by a factor of almost twelve. What the country wants now isn't fuel to see but fuel to move, and to meet the need a scientist at Standard of Indiana explores a chemical process called thermal cracking, which increases the gasoline yield from crude oil. Thermal cracking is hazardous—it exposes oil to very high temperatures and extreme pressure—and during Rockefeller's tenure the chemist who pioneered the idea was told not to pursue it. But after the breakup, newly independent directors give the chemist a go-ahead. The technique succeeds, which means Standard of Indiana can now sextuple the amount of gasoline it makes from each barrel of crude. The company rushes gasoline into America's blossoming auto market. In the mid-twentieth century, this market is still shaped by the monopoly's ghost. Breaking up the company along geographic lines means each small giant is alone, mostly without competitors.

The industry changes fast: first, when oil is discovered in east Texas; then when the Allies reconfigure the supply chain to support World War II, which requires a hundred times more gasoline than World War I; then again when German U-boats begin targeting American oil tankers, forcing the United States to build enormous new pipelines to avoid shipping oil over water. After the war, the industry keeps expanding. Between 1945 and 1950, the number of cars in America increases by more than 50 percent, and oil companies start looking for new oil reserves outside the country's borders, especially in the Middle East. Between 1948 and 1972, oil production throughout the world increases by almost 400 percent, and in the Middle East by more than a thousand percent. In 1958, Standard Oil of Indiana begins importing oil from Iran. Extraction from the Middle East is followed by extraction from North and West Africa, and soon after, for the first time, most gasoline consumed in the United States is refined from foreign oil. The industry's geography has changed and its scale has changed and the importance of Pennsylvania recedes. But the dynamic that Tarbell cared about persists: a few companies have amassed tremendous power, and each decision they make reverberates down to the working class, to each distributor, trucker, attendant, and motorist filling their tank. Which is all to say that in 1965, my grandfather Jim gets a job at a gas station in southeast Iowa. Two years later, he opens his own station. The station is a Standard Oil. Jim is twenty-six.

I started reading about Standard Oil because I wanted context about the business my parents ran for nearly twenty years, the business my grandparents ran before that, the station where I worked as a teenager, where my brother and cousins and aunt and uncle worked. The station was first a Standard, then an Amoco, then a BP. Amoco was how Standard Oil of Indiana rebranded in 1985, the word abbreviated from American Oil Company. In 1998, Amoco merged with BP, which had risen out of Standard Oil of Ohio, the merger effectively recombining two pieces of Rockefeller's empire. I remember Mom's reluctance when Amoco's red, white, and blue color scheme was replaced with the green and white of British Petroleum. Amoco used patriotic colors because Standard Oil of Indiana had passed them down, which meant they were passed down to us; these colors and iconography were part of our household for as long as I can remember. Toy Amoco fuel trucks decorate the home where I grew up. There are miniature Amoco fuel dispensers, tchotchkes from Standard Oil, remembrances of when Grandpa Jim owned the gas station on the corner of town. Standard Oil eventually replaced its crown logo with a torch. It adopted red, white, and blue. Blue for the base of the torch and red for the fire. Fire centers the image. Fire is why it began.

The History of the Standard Oil Company is the best book of journalism I've ever read. Tarbell writes with precision, drama, generosity, scrutiny, and moral clarity. The book is a page-turner. You should read it. Come for the discriminatory transportation rebates and stay for the bribes, the court challenges, the shifting alliances and scientific breakthroughs and passion and despair. I like the sense of dramatic irony that comes with reading her takedown of Rockefeller, knowing how important the story will be after its release, knowing the effect it has. My reading is also narcissistic. I want to know how the history leads to me, and I can't help but notice every reference to Iowa. Early in the book, for example, Tarbell is describing the race to transform western Pennsylvania into a center for the new oil industry, how hundreds of side industries had to spring up to support it:

> A young Iowa schoolteacher and farmer, visiting at his home in Erie County, went to the region. Immediately he saw his chance. It was to invent a receptacle which would hold oil in quantities. Certain large producers listened to his scheme and furnished money to make a trial tank. It was a success, and before many months the schoolteacher was buying thousands of feet of lumber, employing scores of men, and working them and himself—day and night. For nearly ten years he built these wooden tanks. Then seeing that iron tanks—huge receptacles holding thousands of barrels where his held hundreds—were bound to supersede him, he turned, with the ready adaptability which characterized the men of the region, to producing oil for others.

It's an odd choice for Tarbell to avoid naming someone. Telling the story of the oil business, she names every stockholder, marketer, builder, inventor, politician, and judge, but this man from Iowa she simply calls the schoolteacher. Because he is from Iowa I immediately want to know more about him, so I start scouring the internet, before I realize the obvious. The man is from Erie County. He is a builder of wooden oil tanks. He taught school in Iowa. She is writing about her father.

. . . .

Inseparable from my family identity is a corporate identity. In one photo, I'm barely a year old. My brother, who is three, holds me on the couch in our family living room. It's 1989. The flash illuminates our faces and darkens the picture's margins. We smile at the camera. We're wearing jeans and little baby work shirts. I'm sitting on my brother's lap, so my shirt is more visible, blue through the torso with red sleeves. Embroidered on the left breast is the Standard Oil logo. The blue torch and red flame.

In a later photo, I'm sixteen and our family poses with one of Dad's tow trucks. By now Standard has become Amoco has become BP. The truck's cab is white and the door is branded with BP's yellow and green "sunburst," an icon meant to associate BP with renewable energy. BP calls the logo Helios, after the sun god. The photo is set in my hometown's Sunset Park, just down the street from our gas station. The truck angles away from the camera to add a sense of depth. I am leaning against the truck's front fender, one thumb hooked into the front pocket of my jeans because the photographer, Jeff, told me to do that. My brother kneels in the grass, a thumb hooked into his front pocket. Mom stands by the truck's open door and Dad up by the driver seat. We are each dressed in a dark blue BP sweatshirt and denim jeans. No one has a convincing smile. Dad isn't smiling at all. The rest of us are smiling sort of. The smiles are hedged. The vibe is semiformal, which makes sense. It'd be insensitive to appear overjoyed while standing beside a truck that has hauled away sedans and sport utility vehicles whose owners died driving them. We are posing with a disaster-response vehicle. We are standing and kneeling in a park. Some of us are teenagers who complained mercilessly about posing for the photo at all. But here we are making an effort. Sun glints off the truck's emergency lights.

My parents haven't vacationed in twenty years. The only trip that almost counts is a long weekend in New Orleans. They visit me while I'm on pass from Camp Shelby, where my National Guard unit is training for a deployment to Afghanistan. My parents drive from Iowa to Louisiana because Mom worries I might be killed and she'll never see me again. It's a big deal for them to leave the gas station even for this amount of time. Four days. But even this isn't a vacation. It's a going-away. The whole thing is super depressing. At a restaurant, Mom orders a drink with tequila in it, which she never does, and it saddens me because Mom is drinking tequila only to be a good sport about our little trip which she is doing only because she wonders if I'm going to die.

We are trying to make the best of it. We decide to explore a little. One day, Dad guides our rental car along the Gulf Coast. Oil still slicks the water. In April, five months earlier, BP's Deepwater Horizon exploded, killing eleven people. The rig sank thirty-six hours later, and the drill site began hemorrhaging oil. In May, Congress pressured BP into sharing its live feed of the spill site, then pressured the company further to release more angles, so millions of people could observe in real time, from twelve different cameras, the largest environmental disaster in American history. NBC called the video of gushing oil and gas "hypnotic," like a "Yule log." The day after the explosion, hours before the rig sank, the *New York Times* reported, "Officials said the pollution was considered minimal so far because most of the oil and gas was being burned up in the fire." A BP official added, "But that does have the potential to change." BP's name soon becomes synonymous with the catastrophe, and Greenpeace launches a competition encouraging artists to redesign the BP logo in response to the disaster. Submissions include these:

> Beyond Promises, with a sunburst shattered into pieces
> Beyond Pollution, with a sunburst spouting oil
> Beyond Profit, with a green mouth vomiting oil
> Barbarian Practices, with a sunburst made into the teeth of a mouth drooling oil
> Blooming Propaganda
> Blackened Planet
> Bunch of Pricks
> A sunburst overlayed with the biohazard symbol
> A sunburst made into the devil
> Half a sunburst as the hat for a black skull
> A white guy dressed in a white shirt against a white background pouring a quart of oil over his face

Dad drives our rented automobile along the coast. We see a BP sign torn from its platform, the logo smashed into hard-plastic shards. I don't remember anyone saying anything, though I can imagine a conversation where Mom asks about the sign and Dad admits people are angry but implies the anger is out of proportion. The anger at BP has already prompted defensiveness and backlash. When President Obama criticizes BP for its handling of the disaster, a Kentucky Republican running for senate, Rand Paul, describes the criticism as "really un-American" and part of a "blame-game society." He says accidents happen. It's not always someone's fault. The notion of accountability becomes increasingly controversial. Dad drives our rented automobile. The mood is already heavy. The pass ends. In June, on my unit's outpost in rural Afghanistan, I wade into a burn pit and splash gasoline from a jug onto used oil cans and meal trash and dead batteries, light a piece of toilet paper on fire, toss it into the heap, and stand in the pit to stoke the trash until the fire really starts to go, then I hurry out as thick black smoke pours into the sky.

. . . .

Tarbell sees herself as a defender of good business. Rockefeller sees her as an anarchist. He likes to call her a "socialist and anarchist," as if both things could be true at the same time. Really though, Tarbell is not a socialist or an anarchist or even a committed progressive. She scrutinizes Rockefeller's capitalism because she loves the system he is perverting and wants to defend its purer version. She writes about revolutionary women because she is exploring her ideas about women in politics, trying to decide for herself if women should be allowed to vote. She writes *The History of the Standard Oil Company* in the very early years of the twentieth century, with zero interest in the environmental damage caused by oil drilling. In one passage, about Rockefeller's attempts to control oil producers and the producers' failed attempt to resist him by limiting the supply of oil, Tarbell writes, "It seemed as if Nature, outraged that her generosity should be so manipulated as to benefit only the few, had opened her veins to flood the earth with oil, so that all men might know that here was a light cheap enough for the poorest of them." This is an amazing, ridiculous sentence. At least to my modern thinking, which has me noticing the way *generosity* frames the environment as a consenting, enthusiastic agent in its own pillaging. How the environment turns sentient to share Tarbell's fury about the corruption of a capitalist system. How this anthropomorphized, feminized nature, to show her disapproval, starts extracting the oil from herself, in tremendous volumes, just to make a moral point about fairness. Tarbell is obsessed with fairness, but environmental exploitation never figures in her calculus. Tarbell assumes nature is a capitalist, like her.

Mostly though, I'm in awe of her work, partly because she is so morally sure of herself. Tarbell can see a better version of the oil industry, and she writes toward that version. She knows which behaviors are right and wrong. She knows Rockefeller is destroying people's lives, but she also knows that some of the accusations against him are fabricated. He never burned down his rivals' refineries. Tarbell is firm on that. She has the court records and she's considered the evidence. She determines Rockefeller is not an arsonist. She admits he is a compassionate, empathetic man: "There was no more faithful Baptist in Cleveland than he. Every enterprise of that church he had supported liberally from his youth. He gave to its poor. He visited its sick. He wept with its suffering." She goes on, praising his frugality, charity, and humility. Then she makes the turn: "Yet he was willing to strain every nerve to obtain for himself special and unjust privileges from the railroads which were bound to ruin every man in the oil business not sharing them with him." Embedded in the text is a moral tension where Tarbell wants Rockefeller to have been a better industry leader. He is *almost* a hero. She *almost* has me rooting for him, cheering for his ingenuity. He is a brilliant, intuitive general. But something is not quite right in the conduct of the war, a flaw in the ethics of the slaughter. And it's this sense of almost, something nearly right having gone wrong, I think, that requires Tarbell to engage, continuously, her capacity for both horror and amazement. When Standard Oil moves to dominate the refineries in Cleveland, she says the action is "as dazzling an achievement as it was a hateful one."

Tarbell described leaving the religious lectures "fascinated, horror-stricken, confused." She learned to dismantle the confusion. She learned, or rather helped invent, the painstaking craft of modern investigative journalism. What's left after the confusion is the horrific and fascinating, the horrific and amazing, the hateful and dazzling. Tarbell is a writer of the sublime.

. . . .

As a teenager, I work at our family's gas station on the edge of town. I earn five dollars an hour. I pump gas. I check oil and tire pressure. I work the register and scrub mosquito guts from windshields and refill syrup into the soda fountain and refill powder into the cappuccino machine and promise everyone they just bought the winning lotto ticket. Yellow "Support Our Troops" magnets get blown off in the car wash, and I collect them into a pile beneath the counter. Dad has a commercial on the local radio station boasting about the cleanliness of the store's bathrooms, so I have to clean them frequently. People remark on their way to the bathroom, *I heard they're really clean*, and on their way out, *Yeah, that's clean*. At night, I imagine walking into the bathroom and discovering a dead body. Police dramas always start like that, with some ordinary person going about their boring life and discovering a crime scene. I feel like that ordinary person. I eat the leftover donuts, the leftover pizza, the leftover hot dogs, the leftover cookies. Customers like to ask how old is the coffee, as if they have strict rules about coffee freshness, but no matter how alarming my answer it never dissuades someone from pouring a cup.

In the mornings when Dad and I go into the station at the same time, we ride together. He detours the Bronco through the still-dark streets so he can review the gas prices of every other station in town. He understands that nobody pays attention to the price of Mountain Dew but they'll go out of their way to save nine cents on a tank of gas. Dad knows people are sensitive about gasoline. They monitor price fluctuations and drill into them for deeper meanings. People talk about the price of gas like they talk about the weather. It's a glimpse. It's the universe made knowable. It's a way of understanding place and time. It's also a decision he makes each day. Sometimes he chooses a price where he profits one or two cents per gallon and sometimes he breaks even and sometimes he profits if you pay cash but breaks even after a credit card fee and sometimes he sells for a loss no matter the currency because one other station is selling for a loss which forces his hand and he tries to make up the margin on Marlboro Lights and Red Bull. There is an entire cooler now stocked with Red Bull, Monster, Rockstar, Amp, and NOS. These are the new fuels. People used to drink coffee, Dad says once while I'm restocking. It tastes better, and it was cheaper. Fifty cents a cup. Then he shrugs and grins, like isn't the world funny, and walks away.

Once, he's working the counter and I'm standing nearby, being unhelpful, when a customer asks if any BP gasoline is made from Iraqi oil. I don't know the year exactly. Sometime between 2003 and 2005. Few people in our town believe the war in Iraq is about oil; the war, of course, is about the same thing all wars are about, American freedom, but the man across the counter understands that the war for American freedom is taking place in a setting where its consequences might entangle with American consumer products, entangle with our everyday choices and routines. Dad, confidently, says no. BP doesn't get its oil from Iraq. I watch the exchange. I wonder how he knows, if there is a corporate newsletter with an FAQ section or approved talking points. If he has memorized a list of countries the oil does come from. The customer nods, satisfied. From what I can tell now, Dad is not correct. BP's involvement with Iraqi oil dates to at least 1920. The company claims partial responsibility for discovering, in 1953, Iraq's Rumaila oil field, one of the largest oil fields in the world. BP remains today the largest stakeholder in Rumaila and now shares ownership in the Iraq Petroleum Company, which officially discovered the "super-giant" field. BP claims to have been involved in Rumaila since its beginning and throughout its history, a history which includes, in 1991, a dispute between Iraq and Kuwait that provoked the Gulf War. And it seems technically possible that the gasoline being sold at our station in 2003 or 2005 didn't originate with Iraqi oil. It seems technically possible that Dad could know this for sure. But I know, and knew even then, that the question is about broader complicity. Is BP involved in all this? Are we, as consumers, involved, right here and now? If so, how? Standing farther down the counter, I feel relieved at Dad's response, relieved our family business is unrelated to the violence on the other side of the world. How lucky we're always on the right side of things.

On Saturday nights I close the store at ten and drive straight to a friend's house to consume grain alcohol. I wear my BP sweatshirt, which still smells like gasoline. I drink and drink. I love being drunk. It's wonderful. We're all so much more ourselves, it seems. My friend Sam has this bit when he gets really wasted where he takes people aside and asks them to recount their most pressing life problems, and he listens and provides emotional counsel like he's a therapist. The person lies back on a couch and slurs out their problem and Sam offers thoughtful, constructive feedback. Later, Sam goes to graduate school and becomes a therapist. Carson joins the army and misses graduation because he's in South Korea. Nick becomes a police officer. Jesse becomes a valet. Anna becomes a nurse. Manuel joins the marines. Jenny gets involved in a health-focused multilevel marketing scheme. Brian works at a company that designs back-end interfaces for insurance companies. Or some shit like that. He doesn't want to talk about it. We're at a coffee shop in Des Moines catching up. We're in our early thirties, approximately the age when Ida Tarbell beat it for Paris. Brian tells me about his work and then says, Do you really want to hear about this? To be fair, I don't. And I don't want to talk about my shit either. The nice thing about working in nonprofit administration is people forget what you do as soon as you tell them, so writing is what they remember instead. They just think you're a writer, which is cool. At the beginning of our conversation Brian asks if I have a day job or if writing pays for everything and I almost spit out my coffee and all my teeth.

. . . .

Tarbell writes a lot about work. Her autobiography *All in the Day's Work* was published in 1939, five years before her death. In it, she describes leaving her first magazine job:

> I had the American notion that the chief economic duty of the poor
> was to become well-to-do. The laborer, the clerk, the man who
> worked for others should save his money, put it into the business, or
> start out for himself, no matter how hard, how meager the return.
> Dignity and success lay in being your own master, owning your own
> home—I am sure my father would have rather grubbed corn meal
> and bacon from a piece of stony land which was his own than have
> had all the luxuries on a salary.

The contradiction bugs me. Should the poor become wealthier, or should they become entrepreneurs? Is their *chief economic duty* to progress in class or to progress in their independence? If independence confines someone to a poor life, have they failed a duty or achieved a dignity? Tarbell admits she has never been rich or poor, only "well-to-do," which seems to mean upper-middle class. She sees richness, and the continuous pursuit of richness, as an expression of American excellence. In *The History of the Standard Oil Company*, she writes, "The ethical cost of all this is the deep concern. We are a commercial people. We cannot boast of our arts, our crafts, our cultivation; our boast is in the wealth we produce." The *we* here is the nation, the United States, which is too young for robust cultural traditions. We don't make art. We make money.

When Grandpa Jim died in 2020, his obituary stated, "Jim believed in an honest day's work for an honest day's pay." It's a capstone sentence, concluding a paragraph about his years operating the Standard Oil station, about community involvement, about attending the Methodist church, about sports and hunting and all the ways he spent his time. Inside this version of honesty, I think, is an implication of the physical, the demanding—exhaustion conferring moral value. You have to get out there. You have to sweat, walk, grip, bend, stand, kneel, lift. You have to be tired at the end. And you can either be tired for someone else or you can be tired on your own terms, which makes me think Tarbell would've admired Grandpa Jim for opening his own Standard Oil station. After two years working at someone else's station, he made his own path. Conversely, though, I doubt Grandpa would've understood Tarbell leaving a steady job to move to Paris. I think he'd see that as taking the independence thing too far. She wasn't yet a professional writer. She didn't know what she was doing. She just went. She gave up her paycheck and abandoned her family. She left it all because she believed so much in freedom, because she wanted the work to belong to her.

I want independence too, though not always in the same ways as Tarbell, who, true to her word, never married. Jessica and I marry at a hotel ballroom overlooking downtown Iowa City. We create a slideshow for the guests to watch, with photos of our childhoods, including me as an infant in the Standard Oil work shirt and my family in matching BP sweatshirts, then photos of Jessica, then photos of us together, and this next part is hard to explain in retrospect but the love song we dance to waxes nostalgic for manual labor. The song's narrator wishes that instead of becoming a singer he had learned a trade, maybe for the railroad. Like a truer version of him exists doing a difficult job with calloused hands. Later the song is about love, but first it's about roughness, and maybe we choose it because I'm more comfortable dancing publicly to a love song if part of the love is for work. Maybe I see myself as both versions of the narrator, the person he is and the person he wants to have been. He wants to have gone to California, and soon we are that version too. Three months after the wedding we move to San Francisco. We are trying to start out for ourselves, which is possible only because the government paid my college tuition. Because during the deployment, the government bought my clothes and food and paid my rent. I arrived home with $45,738.48. I am twenty-four years old and comparatively well-to-do. Having coffee with Brian in Des Moines, he admits he and our friends shared judgments amongst themselves about me moving to one of the most expensive zip codes in the country. *Lah-dee-dah. Someone has money.* It's true. So we go. Jessica and I each work office jobs at tech start-ups in the Financial District. I spend eighteen months commuting to the Shell Building, named for one of the few oil companies in the United States that was never part of Rockefeller's empire. The Standard Oil Building is two blocks away. Twitter is seven blocks away. Salesforce is three. Power looks different, but it's still power.

One day I'm standing in the break room at my new company, listening to my coworkers—software engineers trained at Google and Microsoft—praise the comedy of their favorite television show, *30 Rock*. I speak up to disagree. I hate that show. What's the point? I tell them the show is designed to make people feel good about Goliath corporations, because see, a Goliath corporation made *this*, and we like this, and isn't it funny how the Goliath satirizes its own brute muscle?

My coworkers think I'm a bummer.

The truth is, I'm a bummer.

Eventually, I come around. I think the show is funny. The show is a riot. I watch its opening credits hundreds of times never realizing until recently how the eponymous *rock* refers to a building that refers to a person, the *rock* refers to a Baptist named John who never burned his rivals' refineries but who strained every nerve to obtain for himself unjust privileges, who broke the law *with fervor* to amass money and power, and I am thinking about what it takes to swipe at that kind of power. It probably doesn't matter why Ida wrote the book, if she felt bitter about her father's struggle or if she was a socialist and anarchist or if she simply took an assignment from a magazine and did a really good job. What matters more than *why* is *how*. The *how* is what counts: She had to push her brother into that stream. She had to buy the microscope. She had to seek the beginning of life, then quit so she could seek something else. She had to scour the archives. She had to study Madame Roland, who was technically a moderate, hated by all the radicals and still beheaded for being too radical. Ida had to get from Titusville to Paris and back. She had to take an interest in rocks, then leaves, then people, then workers, then unfair transportation rebates affecting the shipment of a resource extracted from rocks. She had to arrive in the world among *those* rocks.

Imagine the stamina.

No one believed Ida could start over at thirty-three. She wasn't old, but people treated her like she was. No one believed she could do it except her father, who knew about starting over. The Iowa schoolteacher who walked 800 miles back home and still had some strength left, which was good because there was more work to do. The work had barely started. That's what I mean by stamina. Ida chose to study the revolutionaries. She chose to study the people who fought back, which was good because there was more fighting to do.

. . . .

In the summer, my grandparents hire my brother and cousins and me to paint. We're young, and they want to teach us about work, so we paint their barn and outbuildings. We paint Adirondack chairs and a hay wagon. We paint the station's curbs and islands, the post that holds the Amoco sign. At summer's end we line up at the door to Grandpa's office in the back of the station to get paid. Grandpa is tall and strong and distinctive. Big long ears swing out from the side of his head. He whistles the same bright tune every time he walks out onto the drive, where he is invincibly good at small talk because he knows everything that's happening for a twenty-five-mile radius, and whatever he doesn't know he wants you to tell him about so he can assure you it is the most important thing to have ever happened. We wait for him to call us in. His office adjoins the mechanic bay, where a swimsuit calendar hangs over the work bench, where tires line a rack above the tool chest, where a deep tub allows Grandpa and Dad to find tire punctures—they dunk the tire so bubbles reveal the location of escaping air, and the first time Dad shows me this method I think it's genius, applying the physical world back unto itself like that. My brother and cousins and I wait, then enter the office one by one. Grandpa gives us each several twenty-dollar bills, and then in the mechanic bay he prepares a shallow pan with gasoline and we dip rags into the liquid and wash the paint from our skin. Most days we scrub with hot water, but on the last day we always wash like this. The gasoline smells pungent but it's clear, and bathing with it makes the paint vanish, and now the odor reminds me of that sometimes, the days we spent trying to prove we were honest.

ACKNOWLEDGMENTS

Thank you to Erica Trabold, Verity Sayles, Mara Anspaugh-Lubans, and Maggie Anderson for reading early drafts of these essays. This book wouldn't exist without your energy, patience, and insights. Many thanks to George Estreich for giving such thoughtful feedback on the manuscript.

My sincerest gratitude to the Corvallis-Benton County Public Library. For keeping it all going during tough times. And for letting me borrow so many books. Thank you also to Book Bin and Grass Roots Books and Music for all the special orders and for your tremendous support of local authors.

Thank you to the many independent and university presses out there doing amazing and often underappreciated work. Special thanks to Belt Publishing and the University of Illinois Press for keeping in print the writing of Ida Tarbell.

I'm extremely grateful to Lucas Church and the incredible team at the University of North Carolina Press. Thank you thank you thank you for your amazing work and support.

Thank you to the literary magazines in which some of these essays previously appeared: the *Normal School, Mud Season Review*, and *Iron Horse Literary Review*.

Also a shout-out to the wonderful authors I've never met but whose books I kept close while writing this book because your work inspires me: Amy Fusselman, J. D. Daniels, Aisha Sabatini Sloan, Tracy K. Smith, and Lidia Yuknavitch. Whenever I couldn't figure out a rhythm, I borrowed one from one of you. Thanks.

Thank you to the teachers who populate this book and to the many more teachers, formal and otherwise, who've been so amazingly generous with their time.

Most of all, thank you, Jessica. Always.

WORKS CITED

WHERE I WAS FROM

Didion, Joan. *Where I Was From: A Memoir*. New York: Vintage, 2003.

THE PROBLEM OF LANDING

Biss, Eula. "The Pain Scale." In *Touchstone Anthology of Contemporary Creative Nonfiction*, edited by Lex Williford and Michael Martone, 38. New York: Touchstone, 2007.

Fink, Deborah. *Cutting into the Meatpacking Line: Workers and Change in the Rural Midwest*. Chapel Hill: University of North Carolina Press, 1998.

Gabriel, Trip. "In Iowa, Trump Voters Are Unfazed by Controversies." *New York Times*, January 12, 2017. www.nytimes.com/2017/01/12/us/donald-trump-iowa-conservatives.html.

Gude, Shawn. "Iowa Was Obama's Jump-Start." *Politico*, May 16, 2008. www.politico.com/story/2008/05/iowa-was-obamas-jump-start-010403.

IowaFilmmakers. "Iowa Nice." YouTube video, 1:50, January 12, 2012. www.youtube.com/watch?v=qLZZ6JDog9Y.

Jett, Tyler. "Family of Tyson Employee in Iowa Who Died of COVID-19 Sues Company, Alleging Gross Negligence." *Des Moines Register*, October 6, 2020. www.desmoinesregister.com/story/money/business/2020/10/06/tyson-foods-sued-over-columbus-junction-workers-covid-19-death-iowa/3636300001/.

———. "In New Allegation, Lawsuit Says Tyson Officials Lied to Interpreters about COVID-19 Dangers in Waterloo Plant." *Des Moines Register*, November 30, 2020. www.desmoinesregister.com/story/money/business/2020/11/30/lawsuit-tyson-managers-lied-interpreters-covid-19-threat-waterloo-iowa-plant/6464310002/.

Kendzior, Sarah. *The View from Flyover Country: Dispatches from the Forgotten America*. New York: Flatiron Books, 2015.

Klein, Joe. "The Fresh Face." *Time*, October 2006. http://content.time.com/time/subscriber/article/0,33009,1546362,00.html. (Print version title: "Why Barack Obama Could Be the Next President").

O'Gieblyn, Meghan. *Interior States: Essays*. New York: Anchor Books, 2018.

Rankine, Claudia. *Just Us: An American Conversation*. Minneapolis: Graywolf Press, 2020.

Smarsh, Sarah. *Heartland: A Memoir of Working Hard and Being Broke in the Richest Country on Earth*. New York: Scribner, 2018.

Winfrey-Harris, Tamara. "Stop Pretending Black Midwesterners Don't Exist." In *Black in the Middle: An Anthology of the Black Midwest*, edited by Terrion L. Williamson, 169. Cleveland: Belt Publishing, 2020.

CENTRAL CROSSINGS

City of Iowa City. *Downtown and Riverfront Crossings Master Plan*. Report. Iowa City, January 2013.

————. *Riverfront Crossings District Sub-area Plan*. Report. Iowa City, April 2011.

Miller, Greg. "New Map Reveals Ships Buried below San Francisco." *National Geographic*, June 1, 2017. www.nationalgeographic.com/history/article/map -ships-buried-san-francisco.

Rimel, Anthony. "Suspect in Custody after Corvallis Foster Farms Incident; No Injuries Reported." *Corvallis (Ore.) Gazette-Times*, August 29, 2019. www.gazettetimes.com /news/local/suspect-in-custody-after-corvallis-foster-farms-incident-no-injuries -reported/article_93a69906a-08d1–5c22-bb0c-e3b0546fac06.html.

Schulz, Kathryn. "The Really Big One." *New Yorker*, July 13, 2015. www.newyorker.com /magazine/2015/07/20/the-really-big-one.

Van Derbeken, Jaxon, Demian Bulwa, and Erin Allday. "SF Plane Crash: Crew Tried to Abort Landing." *San Francisco Chronicle*, July 7, 2013. www.sfgate.com/bayarea /article/SF-plane-crash-Crew-tried-to-abort-landing-4650990.php.

TRUE NORTH

"The 1840s in Benton County." Benton County Historical Society and Museum. Accessed May 13, 2022. www.bentoncountymuseum.org/index.php/research /benton-county-history/the-1840s.

"The 1850s in Benton County." Benton County Historical Society and Museum. Accessed May 13, 2022. www.bentoncountymuseum.org/index.php/research /benton-county-history/the-1850s.

"American Indians and Westward Expansion." State Historical Society of Iowa. Accessed May 13, 2022. https://iowaculture.gov/history/education/educator -resources/primary-source-sets/westward-expansion-and-native-americans.

"Bellfountain: Local History in the Special Collections and Archives Research Center." Oregon State University Libraries. Last modified April 22, 2022. https://guides .library.oregonstate.edu/localhistory/bellfountain.

Bennett, Mary, Lantz Buffalo, Dawn Suzanne Wanatee, and State Historical Society of Iowa. "Meskwaki History." Iowa City: State Historical Society of Iowa, 2004.

Biss, Eula. Interview with Jeffery Gleaves. *Harper's Magazine*, October 1, 2014. https:// harpers.org/2014/10/discussing-on-immunity-an-inoculation-with-eula-biss.

"Black in Oregon, 1840–1870." Oregon Secretary of State. Accessed May 13, 2022. https://sos.oregon.gov/archives/exhibits/black-history/Pages/context/chronology .aspx.

"Body Cam Footage: Genesis Hansen Arrest." *Corvallis Gazette-Times* video, October 22, 2019. www.gazettetimes.com/news/local/body-cam-footage-genesis-hansen-arrest /youtube_4c22c99c-7194–5a1b-934c-9084da7ae7ba.html.

Brown, DeNeen L. "When Portland Banned Blacks: Oregon's Shameful History as an 'All-White' State." *Washington Post*, June 7, 2017. www.washingtonpost .com/news/retropolis/wp/2017/06/07/when-portland-banned-blacks-oregons -shameful-history-as-an-all-white-state/.

Crucet, Jennine Capó. *My Time among the Whites: Notes from an Unfinished Education.* New York: Picador, 2019.

Flaccus, Gillian. "In Oregon, Stark Rural-Urban Divide Fuels Climate Dispute." Associated Press, June 26, 2019. www.registerguard.com/story/news/2019 /06/26/in-oregon-stark-rural-urban/4825247007.

Jackson, Mitchell. Interview with David Naimon. *Between the Covers.* Podcast audio, March 18, 2019. https://tinhouse.com/podcast/mitchell-s-jackson-survival -math.

Jordan Schnitzer Museum of Art. "Why Aren't There More Black People in Oregon? A Hidden History." A Conversation with Walidah Imarisha. YouTube video, 1:45:32, May 6, 2014. www.youtube.com/watch?v=DWC-8hvP7aY.

Kurtz, Nettie Ray. *Diary.* Edited by Judy Watts. Self-published, Bookemon, 2018.

Lorde, Audre. *Sister Outsider: Essays and Speeches.* Freedom, CA: Crossing Press, 1984.

"Many Voters Opt to Keep Racist Language in Constitution." Associated Press, November 7, 2002. https://tdn.com/news/state-and-regional/many-voters-opt -to-keep-racist-language-in-constitution/article_d1bea75e-4398–55bb-8f0b -eea4e9df5ad9.html.

"The Path to Statehood." Iowa PBS. Accessed May 13, 2022. www.iowapbs.org /iowapathways/mypath/2668/path-statehood.

Rich, Adrienne. *The Fact of a Doorframe: Selected Poems, 1950–2001.* New York: W. W. Norton, 2002.

"Sac & Fox Tribe of the Mississippi in Iowa." Meskwaki Nation, May 6, 2022. www.meskwaki.org/history/.

Slaughter, William B. *Reminiscences of Distinguished Men, with an Autobiography.* Milwaukee: Godfrey and Crandall, Printers and Publishers, 1878.

Smith, Stacey L., Thomas Bahde, Stephen Dow Beckham, Marisa Chappell, and Dwaine Plaza. *Historical Reports on OSU Building Names.* Corvallis: Oregon State University, October 16, 2017.

"A Timeline of Iowa History." Iowa History Online. Accessed May 13, 2022. https:// iowaonline.uni.edu.

Tuttle, Charles R., and Daniel S. Durrie. *An Illustrated History of the State of Iowa, Being a Complete Civil, Political, and Military History of the State, from Its First Exploration Down to 1875.* Chicago: Richard S. Peale and Company, 1876.

Union Historical Company. *The History of Washington County, Iowa, Containing a History of the County, Its Cities, Towns, &c.* Des Moines: Union Historical Company, 1880.

"A Very Lucky Argument to Lose." CBS News, August 22, 2001. www.cbsnews.com /news/a-very-lucky-argument-to-lose/.

DISTANCE FROM THE QUESTION, OR NOTES
ON BEING ASKED ABOUT A WAR

Ackerman, Elliot. "A Battle in Falluja, Revisited." *New York Times*, May 26, 2019. www.nytimes.com/2019/05/25/opinion/memorial-day-falluja.html.

"Army Investigates National Guard Recruiting Program Fraud." *Dallas Morning News*, February 4, 2014. www.dallasnews.com/news/2014/02/05/army -investigates-national-guard-recruiting-program-fraud/.

Bhagwati, Anuradha. *Unbecoming: A Memoir of Disobedience*. New York: Atria Books, 2019.

Filkins, Dexter. *The Forever War*. New York: Vintage, 2008.

Fugett, Karie. "Unusual Objects." *Doctor T. J. Eckleburg Review*, February 5, 2019. www.eckleburg.org/unusual-objects-by-karie-fugett/.

Kiernan, Steven. "The Difference between Us." *Kenyon Review Online*, December 2017. https://kenyonreview.org/kr-online-issue/2017-novdec/selections /steven-kiernan-342846.

Klay, Phil. *Redeployment*. New York: Penguin, 2014.

One Day at a Time. Season 1, episode 1, "This Is It." Directed by Pamela Fryman. Aired January 6, 2017.

Pham, Drew. "Letters to My Country That She Will Never Read, Part 3." *The War Horse*, September 13, 2018. https://thewarhorse.org/letters-to-my-country -that-she-will-never-read-part-3.

Prifogle, Lizbeth. "To America." In *Incoming: Veteran Writers on Coming Home*, edited by Justin Hudnall, Julia Dixon Evans, and Rolf Yngve, 126–35. San Diego: SSWA Press, 2015.

OF PREROGATIVE!

Clark, Travis. "The 50 Best-Selling Albums of All Time." *Business Insider*, September 22, 2021. www.businessinsider.com/50-best-selling-albums-all-time-2016–9.

"George Strait Album Sales." BestSellingAlbums.org. Accessed May 27, 2022. https:// bestsellingalbums.org/artist/4671.

Jackson, Josh. "The 25 Best-Selling Albums of All Time." *Paste*, August 22, 2018. www .pastemagazine.com/music/best-selling-albums/the-best-selling-albums-of-all-time/.

Thompson, Gayle. "24 Years Ago: Shania Twain's 'Come On Over' Is Released." *The Boot*, November 4, 2021. https://theboot.com/shania-twain-come-on-over-released/.

Tolstoy, Leo. *Anna Karenina*. Translated by Richard Pevear and Larissa Volokhonsky. New York: Penguin, 2000.

Twain, Shania. "Shania Twain—Come On Over (Live)." YouTube video, 3:12. Accessed May 27, 2022. www.youtube.com/watch?v=VNe2cjo3-eA.

AND GRINDING CRY OF DISASTER, OR NOTES ON *HOME IMPROVEMENT*

Diaz, Johnny, Maria Cramer, and Christina Morales. "What to Know about the Death of Vanessa Guillen." *New York Times*, April 30, 2021. www.nytimes.com/article /vanessa-guillen-fort-hood.html.

Faludi, Susan. Interview with Brian Lamb. *Booknotes*. C-SPAN, October 2, 1992. www.c-span.org/video/?33591-1/backlash.

———. *Backlash: The Undeclared War against American Women*. 2020 Broadway Books Trade Paperback Edition. New York: Broadway Books, 2020.

Floorwalker, Mike. "The Reason Wilson from Home Improvement Never Showed His Face." *Looper*, September 13, 2019. www.looper.com/166051/the-reason -wilson-from-home-improvement-never-showed-his-face/.

Ford, George C. "Washington Area Boasts Diverse Industries." *Gazette* (Cedar Rapids, IA), June 14, 2015. www.thegazette.com/news/washington-area-boasts -diverse-industries/.

Home Improvement. "Backstage Pass." DailyMotion, 20:01. Accessed May 27, 2022. www.dailymotion.com/video/x23b1cz.

———. "The Long and Winding Road (Part 3)." DailyMotion, 22:25. Accessed May 27, 2022. www.dailymotion.com/video/x5erjg1.

———. "Stereo-Typical." YouTube video, 21:50. Accessed December 1, 2020. www .youtube.com/watch?v=J_mXNoOcGCA&list=PLbUdxVvIlinc5YJ_MiTtWL -5DaDef6qbg&index=22.

Iowa Biodiesel Board. "Iowa Renewable Energy in Washington, Iowa." YouTube video, 2:25, May 5, 2020. www.youtube.com/watch?v=O8aZ3I8V2wo.

Koestenbaum, Wayne. *Figure It Out: Essays*. New York: Soft Skull Press, 2020.

Michaels, Brandon. "These Wild Home Improvement Fan Theories Are Not as Far-Fetched as You Think." *Ranker*, May 14, 2020. www.ranker.com/list /home-improvement-fan-theories/brandon-michaels.

Oxner, Reese. "Army Report Finds Fort Hood Soldier Vanessa Guillén Reported Being Sexually Harassed Twice Before She Was Killed." *Texas Tribune*, April 30, 2021. www.texastribune.org/2021/04/30/vanessa-guillen-sexual-harassment-fort-hood/.

Reed, Phil. "Modine Closing Its Washington Plant Friday." KCRG-TV9, December 13, 2016. www.kcrg.com/content/news/Modine-closing-its-Washington-plant -Friday-406395955.html.

Urness, Zach. "Oregon's 2020 Wildfire Season Brought a New Level of Destruction. It Could Be Just the Beginning." *Salem Statesman Journal*, October 30, 2020. www.statesmanjournal.com/story/news/2020/10/30/climate-change-oregon -wildfires-2020/6056170002/.

Wenger, Linda. "Crane Valve Foundry to Close." *Southeast Iowa Union*, September 30, 2018. www.southeastiowaunion.com/news/crane-valve-foundry-to-close/.

THE LAST VIDEO STORE ESSAY

Alderman, Naomi. *The Power*. New York: Hachette, 2016.

Associated Press. "Welles' Last Role? Original 'Transformers.'" *Today*, June 22, 2007. www.today.com/popculture/welles-last-role-original-transformers-wbna19378720.

Bach, Trevor. "CBD Helps Revitalize Midwestern Video Chain." *US News*, December 13, 2019. www.usnews.com/news/best-states/articles/2019–12–13 /cbd-is-midwest-video-chains-blockbuster-solution-to-survival.

Boden, Anna, dir. *Captain Marvel*. 2019; Burbank: Walt Disney. www.disneyplus.com/.

City and County of San Francisco. Planning Department. Planning Code, 303.1
　　"Formula Retail Uses." April 15, 2022.

"Family Video in Washington to Close at End of Month." *Southeast Iowa Union*,
　　September 20, 2019. www.southeastiowaunion.com/news/family-video
　　-in-washington-to-close-at-end-of-month/.

Greenwell, Garth. "Making Meaning." *Harper's*, November 2020. https://harpers.org
　　/archive/2020/11/making-meaning-garth-greenwell/.

Herbert, Daniel. *Videoland: Movie Culture at the American Video Store*. Oakland:
　　University of California Press, 2014.

"History of Ratings." Classification and Rating Administration. Accessed May 27, 2022.
　　www.filmratings.com/History.

Hotel, David. "Walmart Supercenter Opens in Washington." *Southeast Iowa Union*,
　　September 30, 2018. www.southeastiowaunion.com/news/walmart-supercenter
　　-opens-in-washington/.

Kirsch, Noah. "The Last Video Chain: The Inside Story of Family Video and Its
　　$400 Million Owner." *Forbes*, February 21, 2017. www.forbes.com/sites
　　/noahkirsch/2017/02/21/the-last-video-chain-the-inside-story-of-family-video
　　-and-its-400-million-owner/?sh=60068926da60.

Moore, John, dir. *Behind Enemy Lines*. 2001; Los Angeles: Twentieth Century Fox, 2002.
　　DVD.

"Netflix: Number of Employees 2010–2022." MacroTrends. Accessed May 27, 2022.
　　www.macrotrends.net/stocks/charts/NFLX/netflix/number-of-employees.

Reed, Peyton, dir. *Yes Man*. 2008; Burbank: Warner Bros. Pictures, 2009. DVD.

Shin, Nelson, dir. *Transformers: The Movie*. 1986; Wilmington: De Laurentiis
　　Entertainment Group, 2000. DVD.

Spangler, Todd. "Family Video, Last National Rental Chain, Is Shutting Down All
　　Remaining Stores." *Variety*, January 6, 2021. https://variety.com/2021/digital
　　/news/family-video-shutting-down-all-stores-1234879655/.

Tarantino, Quentin, dir. *Pulp Fiction*. 1994; Los Angeles: Miramax, 1997. DVD.

Tokosh, Joseph, and Xuwei Chen. "The Green and Orange Place That Still Rents
　　Movies: Investigating the Closures of Family Video Movie Stores." *Professional
　　Geographer*, June 12, 2020.

INDEFATIGABLE ZEAL

"The Acquisition of Iowa Lands from the Indians." *Annals of Iowa* 7 (1906): 283–90.

Associated Press. "Rand Paul: Obama BP Criticism 'Un-American.'" NBC News, May
　　21, 2010. www.nbcnews.com/id/wbna37273085.

Brox, Jane. *Brilliant: The Evolution of Artificial Light*. New York: Mariner, 2010.

Daly, Michael. "BP in Rumaila." Transcript of speech delivered at International
　　Petroleum Week, London, February 16, 2010. www.bp.com/genericarticle
　　.do?categoryId=98&contentId=7059849.

"Greenpeace Competition to Redesign the BP Logo." *Guardian*, June 10, 2010.
　　www.theguardian.com/environment/gallery/2010/jun/10/greenpeace-bp
　　-logo-competition.

"A Historic Step in Iraq." BP, July 9, 2010. www.bp.com/sectiongenericarticle
    .do?categoryId=9031310&contentId=7057102.

Nuckols, Ben, and Greg Bluestein. "Oil Spill Cam Becomes Internet Sensation."
    Associated Press, May 28, 2010. www.nbcnews.com/id/wbna37406317.

Robertson, Campbell. "Search Continues after Oil Rig Blast." *New York Times*, April 21,
    2010. www.nytimes.com/2010/04/22/us/22rig.html.

Rosenheim, Daniel. "Goodbye, Standard; Hello, Amoco Corp." *Chicago Tribune*, April
    24, 1985. www.chicagotribune.com/news/ct-xpm-1985–04–24–8501240407-story
    .html.

Sherman, Bill. "Tracing the Treaties: How They Affected American Indians and Iowa."
    Iowa History Journal. Accessed May 27, 2022. http://iowahistoryjournal.com
    /tracing-treaties-affected-american-indians-iowa/.

Tarbell, Ida. *All in the Day's Work: An Autobiography.* Urbana: University of Illinois
    Press, 2003.

———. *The History of the Standard Oil Company.* Cleveland: Belt Publishing, 2018.

Yergin, Daniel. *The Prize: The Epic Quest for Oil, Money and Power.* New York: Free
    Press, 1991.

Printed in the USA
CPSIA information can be obtained
at www.ICGtesting.com
CBHW021721180224
4434CB00001B/114